The Gluten-Free KITCHEN

The Gluten-Free KITCHEN

*Feel-good food for
happy and healthy eating*

This edition published by Parragon Books Ltd in 2016
LOVE FOOD is an imprint of Parragon Books Ltd

Parragon Books Ltd
Chartist House
15–17 Trim Street
Bath BA1 1HA, UK
www.parragon.com/lovefood

Copyright © Parragon Books Ltd 2016

LOVE FOOD and the accompanying heart device is a registered
trademark of Parragon Books Ltd in Australia, the UK, USA,
India and the EU.

ISBN 978-1-4748-1756-1

Printed in China

Introduction written by Fiona Hunter
Cover and new photography on pages 6–18 and
pages 44, 72 and 100 by Tony Briscoe

NOTES FOR THE READER

This book uses both metric and imperial measurements. Follow
the same units of measurement throughout; do not mix metric
and imperial. All spoon measurements are level: teaspoons
are assumed to be 5 ml, and tablespoons are assumed to be
15 ml. Unless otherwise stated, milk is assumed to be full fat,
eggs and individual fruits and vegetables are medium, pepper
is freshly ground black pepper and salt is table salt. A pinch
of salt is calculated as $1/16$ of a teaspoon. Unless otherwise
stated, all root vegetables should be peeled prior to using.

The times given are an approximate guide only. Preparation
times differ according to the techniques used by different
people and the cooking times may also vary from those given.

Please note that any ingredients stated as being optional are
not included in the nutritional values provided. The nutritional
values given are approximate and provided as a guideline
only, they do not account for individual cooks, scales and
portion sizes. The nutritional values provided are per serving
or per item.

While the publisher of the book and the original author(s)
of the recipes and other text have made all reasonable
efforts to ensure that the information contained in this book
is accurate and up to date at the time of publication, anyone
reading this book should note the following important points: –
* Medical and pharmaceutical knowledge is constantly
changing and the author(s) and the publisher cannot and
do not guarantee the accuracy or appropriateness of the
contents of this book;
* In any event, this book is not intended to be, and should not
be relied upon as, a substitute for appropriate, tailored
professional advice. Both the author(s) and the publisher
strongly recommend that a doctor or other healthcare
professional is consulted before embarking on major dietary
changes;
* For the reasons set out above, and to the fullest extent
permitted by law, the author(s) and publisher: (i) cannot
and do not accept any legal duty of care or responsibility in
relation to the accuracy or appropriateness of the contents
of this book, even where expressed as 'advice' or using
other words to this effect; and (ii) disclaim any liability,
loss, damage or risk that may be claimed or incurred as a
consequence – directly or indirectly – of the use and/or
application of any of the contents of this book.

The publisher has been careful to select recipes that contain
gluten-free products. Any ready-made ingredients that
could potentially contain gluten have been listed as gluten
free, so readers know to check they are gluten free.
However, always read labels carefully and, if necessary,
check with the manufacturer.

CONTENTS

WHY GO GLUTEN-FREE?

Coeliac disease, which is the most common reason to follow a gluten-free diet, affects around 1 in 100 adults in the UK. However, it seems that this is just the tip of a very large iceberg, as some experts believe that only one in eight people with the condition are officially diagnosed, which means many more people may have the condition without knowing it.

But coeliac disease isn't the only reason for going gluten-free, and a growing number of people find that eliminating gluten and wheat can be the answer to a whole range of underlying health problems. Some successful sportsmen and women have attributed their improved stamina and energy to the fact that they have cut gluten out of their diets.

So should you try a gluten-free diet? Well, if you experience any of the symptoms listed below then it's certainly worth a try – after all, you've got nothing to lose and much to gain.

For people with coeliac disease, even the tiniest amount of gluten can cause problems. Some people with gluten intolerance find they can eat small amounts from time to time, but when you embark on your gluten-free journey it's best to eliminate all gluten from your diet.

Cutting gluten out of your diet may seem like a daunting task, but you'll find it doesn't have to be hard work and it doesn't mean missing out on your favourite foods. In this book you'll find delicious recipes for favourites such as stuffed peppers, roast chicken and apple pie as well as gluten-free adaptations of other recipes, such as polenta bruschettas, gram flour rolls and sago dessert. We'll help you identify foods you need to avoid and those that might contain hidden gluten, give tips on how to bake with gluten-free flour and explain how to plan healthy, gluten-free meals that you and your whole family can enjoy.

SYMPTOMS ASSOCIATED WITH COELIAC DISEASE AND GLUTEN INTOLERANCE:

~ Digestive problems include diarrhoea and/or constipation
~ Bloating, stomach pain, cramping
~ Unexplained tiredness and lack of energy
~ Headaches and migraine
~ Mouth ulcers
~ Alopecia (hair loss)
~ Skin problems
~ Painful joints

ELIMINATING GLUTEN

Gluten is a protein found in wheat, rye and barley, and in foods such as cakes, pastry, bread and pasta, which are made from these grains. Eliminating gluten from your diet is not as simple as cutting out obvious sources of wheat, such as bread and pasta, because wheat and other gluten-containing grains are often used in other foods.

In some cases food that is naturally gluten-free can become contaminated with gluten during processing or storage. To make sure a food or ingredient is gluten free it's vital to check the label on all processed food, or get advice from a coeliac advice group about choosing suitable products. It's also important to remember that products that are labelled as wheat-free are not necessarily gluten-free, because they may contain grains such as barley or rye.

FOOD AND DRINKS CONTAINING GLUTEN:

~ Wheat, rye, barley and spelt
~ All biscuits, breads, cakes, chapatis, crackers, muffins, pastries, pizza bases, rolls and scones that are made from wheat, rye, spelt or barley flour
~ Wheat noodles and pasta, couscous, semolina, bulgur wheat, faro and freekeh
~ Wheat-based breakfast cereals
~ Meat and poultry cooked in batter or breadcrumbs, such as breaded ham, faggots, haggis, rissoles and Scotch eggs
~ Fish or shellfish coated in batter or breadcrumbs, such as fish cakes and fish fingers
~ Dairy products like fromage frais and yogurt that contain muesli or cereals
~ Vegetables and fruit covered in batter or breadcrumbs, or dusted with flour
~ Potatoes covered in batter or breadcrumbs, or dusted with flour, such as potato croquettes
~ Soy sauce
~ Ice-cream cones and wafers and puddings made using semolina or wheat flour
~ Stuffing made from breadcrumbs
~ Barley water/squash, ale, lager, malted milk and stout

Check the label on all packaged and processed foods. Avoid foods containing the following ingredients unless you know for sure they are gluten-free:

~ Bran, cereal binder, cereal filler, starch, cereal protein, modified starch, edible starch, food starch flour, rusk, rye and vegetable protein.

GLUTEN-FREE ALTERNATIVES

Cutting gluten out of your diet may seem like a massive change, but once you've got a routine in place you will find it doesn't have to be hard work, and you'll quickly discover that gluten-free meals can be just as delicious as those containing gluten.

There are plenty of foods that are naturally gluten-free and food manufacturers have responded to the growing number of people choosing to avoid gluten by producing a range of products such as gluten-free flour, cakes, biscuits, pasta, muffins, ready-made pastry and breads. Of course, you don't need to rely on manufactured gluten-free foods, and some of our recipes include delicious gluten-free cakes, biscuits and breads.

HERE ARE SOME NATURALLY GLUTEN-FREE FOODS:

~ Gluten-free grains and gluten-free flour
  These include amaranth, buckwheat, cassava, chestnut flour, chickpea flour, corn (maize), corn starch, gram flour, millet, mustard flour, polenta (cornmeal), potato flour, potato starch, quinoa, rice, rice bran, rice flour, sago, sorghum, soya flour, starch, tapioca, tapioca starch, teff and urd/urid flour.
~ Meat, poultry, fish and shellfish
~ Fruit and vegetables – canned, dried, fresh, frozen and juiced pure fruits and vegetables are suitable
~ Potatoes, sweet potatoes, rice noodles, soba (buckwheat) noodles (check as not all brands of soba noodles are gluten-free)
~ Nuts and seeds – (check dry-roasted peanuts because they are not always gluten-free)
~ Pulses – all dried and canned beans (baked beans are not usually gluten-free)
~ Dairy products – eggs, cheese, milk, cream, crème fraîche, sour cream, buttermilk, yogurt
~ Butter, cooking oils, ghee, lard, margarine and reduced and low-fat spreads

WHAT ABOUT OATS?

Oats do not contain gluten, but they do contain a similar protein. However, it doesn't seem to cause the same adverse reaction as gluten in wheat and other grains. If you would like to include oats in your diet, start by adding a small amount to see if there is any adverse reaction. Children and people with severe coeliac disease are advised to talk to their doctor or registered dietitian before introducing oats into the diet. Oats are often contaminated with gluten during processing so it's important to make sure you buy oats that are labelled as gluten-free.

THE GLUTEN-FREE KITCHEN

For people with coeliac disease and severe gluten intolerance, even the tiniest amount of gluten can be enough to trigger a reaction. So one of the first things you need to do when you switch to a gluten-free diet is to organise your kitchen to minimize the risk of cross contamination – this is particularly important if you are sharing the kitchen with people who can, and do, eat gluten. You need to create a gluten-free zone.

Just because you can't see gluten it doesn't mean it's not there. So before you start preparing food, wipe down surfaces and wash all pots and pans thoroughly with detergent and hot water. For equipment such as chopping boards, colanders, serving tongs and wooden spoons it's helpful to have a set that are used exclusively for gluten-free cooking – colour coding equipment makes it clear which is gluten-free.

If possible, keep all your gluten-free ingredients in a separate cupboard to keep them away from ingredients containing gluten. Careful labelling will help avoid cross-contamination and keep the kitchen a gluten-free zone. Use labels on jars of gluten-free flour and grains. Sticky notes are also useful so you can label your foods in the fridge if you share your house with other gluten eaters. it is wise to dedicate one shelf in the fridge for gluten-free food – the top shelf is best so you can avoid the risk of something spilling on the food below.

Appliances such as toasters can easily become cross-contaminated with gluten, so it is advisable to keep a separate toaster for gluten-free bread. You can also use toaster bags to prevent contamination. If you are planning on making gluten-free bread, it is worth investing in a breadmaker that you keep for gluten-free bread. If you use a deep-fat fryer, make sure that the oil doesn't become contaminated with gluten by using it to fry food coated with regular breadcrumbs or batter.

Foods like jam and mayonnaise can become contaminated with gluten – if for instance a knife or spoon is used to spread jam on regular bread and then it is dipped back into the jar – so always use clean utensils and encourage your family or house mates to do the same. Another idea is to use squeeze containers or purchase separate jars and label them clearly as gluten free.

Once you've created a gluten-free zone, make sure that everyone else who uses the kitchen understands the importance of keeping things separate.

GLUTEN-FREE BAKING

You're seriously considering a gluten-free diet. You know that there are plenty of gluten-free products on the market, but it's hard to imagine life without the delights of freshly baked bread, sweet and savoury biscuits, scones, muffins and cakes. Well, there is no need for you to make this sacrifice because you can bake your own delicious gluten-free products – it just requires a slightly different approach.

Flour can be made by grinding any grain as well as foods such as beans, nuts and seeds, so there are lots of alternatives to wheat flour – brown rice flour, coconut flour, buckwheat flour and chestnut flour are all naturally gluten-free. The key to success is to select the right flour for the job. Different types of flour have different properties and some can have quite a distinctive flavour, so for baking it's usually better to use a blend of different gluten-free flours, or use one of the commercially prepared blends.

Gluten is what gives bread and baked goods, such as cakes and muffins, their characteristic texture and structure. When flour is mixed with water the gluten becomes elastic, turning the mixture into a soft, stretchy dough that can be kneaded and shaped. Carbon dioxide produced by yeast or baking powder is trapped within the dough and held there by the gluten, producing the characteristic texture of bread and cakes. Products made with gluten-free flour won't have exactly the same texture as those made with wheat flour, but with a little perseverance and practice it is possible to produce excellent gluten-free bread and cakes.

Adding either guar or xanthan gum will help to improve the texture of baked goods and make bread less crumbly and pastry easier to roll. It also improves the shelf life of your baked creations. Bread rolls and loaves made with gluten-free flour don't hold their shape, so it helps to bake them in a loaf or muffin tin. Because gluten is a protein, when you use gluten-free flour it is helpful to add extra protein, so you can try replacing some of the water or fluid with a beaten egg. Not all baking powder brands are gluten-free, so if the recipe you are using requires baking powder check the label – the same goes for any other ingredients you are planning to add.

Lastly, don't expect your first gluten-free bake to be perfect – there are certain things that you'll pick up gradually, such as the need to mix bread dough very thoroughly (the good thing is there is no gluten to be overworked!) and understand the importance of using the exact ingredient proportions stated in a recipe. It is also sensible to avoid experimenting with substituting ingredients until you've had a bit of practice as a gluten-free baker.

GLUTEN-FREE HEALTHY EATING

A gluten-free diet can be a very healthy one because of the emphasis placed on fresh, natural and unprocessed foods. However, it's important to remember that a gluten-free food isn't automatically healthy.

Cakes and biscuits made with gluten-free flour should be a treat rather than a regular part of your diet. Some commercial gluten-free products such as sandwiches, baked goods and ready meals can contain higher levels of fat, salt and or sugar than similar gluten products. If you buy these products regularly, spend a few minutes looking at the nutritional information on the label and consider how healthy the products really are. If you make your own products, you naturally have more control over what you put in.

The damage to the intestine that occurs as a result of untreated coeliac disease can cause malabsorption which can lead to nutritional deficiencies. The vitamins and minerals most likely to be malabsorbed are iron, calcium, zinc and magnesium, so when you start on a gluten-free diet make sure that your diet contains plenty of foods that are rich in these nutrients.

A healthy gluten-free diet should include:
~ At least 5 portions of fruit and/or vegetables a day
~ 2–3 servings/day of lean protein such as lean meat, fish or poultry, beans or pulses
~ 2–3 servings/day of calcium-rich dairy foods such as low or reduced-fat milk, cheese or yogurt
~ Wholegrain, unrefined and fibre-rich, gluten-free carbohydrates such as beans and pulses and
    brown rice
~ Small amounts of healthy unsaturated fats like those found in olive or rapeseed oil and foods like
    oil-rich fish, nuts, seeds and avocado pears

Keep to a minimum:
~ Saturated fats, salt and sugar
~ Foods such as salty snacks, confectionery, cakes biscuits and desserts should be kept as a treat
    rather than a regular part of your diet

So now it's time to start your healthy, gluten-free journey!

BREAKFASTS

Millet porridge with apricot purée	20
Dried fruit compote with quinoa	22
Apple and seed muesli	24
Apple, carrot and cucumber juice	26
Pear, oat and blueberry breakfast loaf	28
Apricot and raisin oat bars	30
Coconut breakfast cookies	32
Blueberry and oatmeal muffins	34
Eggs in peppers and tomato sauce	36
Mushroom röstis	38
Red beetroot hash	40
Broccoli hash	42

MILLET PORRIDGE WITH APRICOT PURÉE

Gluten-free millet makes a good replacement for oats and the significant apricot content will boost your iron intake for the day.

SERVES: 4
PREP: 5 MINS COOK: 25 MINS

225 g/8 oz millet flakes
450 ml/16 fl oz milk
pinch of salt
freshly grated nutmeg, to serve

APRICOT PURÉE
115 g/4 oz dried apricots, roughly chopped
300 ml/10 fl oz water

1. To make the apricot purée, put the apricots into a saucepan and cover with the water. Bring to the boil, then reduce the heat and simmer, half covered, for 20 minutes until the apricots are very tender. Use a hand–held blender or transfer the apricots, along with any water left in the saucepan, to a food processor or blender and process until smooth. Set aside.

2. To make the porridge, put the millet flakes into a saucepan and add the milk and salt. Bring to the boil, then reduce the heat and simmer for 5 minutes, stirring frequently, until cooked and creamy.

3. To serve, spoon into four bowls and top with the apricot purée and a little nutmeg.

APRICOT PURÉE
Use plump, soft apricots to give a smooth and luxurious fruit purée.

PER SERVING: 289 KCALS | 3G FAT | 1G SAT FAT | 52G CARBS | 12G SUGARS | 2.5G FIBRE | 4.5G PROTEIN | 0.6G SALT

DRIED FRUIT COMPOTE WITH QUINOA

Quinoa takes on a sweet, spicy, citrus flavour when simmered with honey, nutmeg and freshly grated orange rind. This breakfast treat is equally delicious as a dessert.

SERVES: 2
PREP: 15 MINS COOK: 20 MINS

75 g/2³⁄₄ oz white quinoa, rinsed
500 ml/18 fl oz water
2 tsp honey
¼ tsp freshly grated nutmeg
finely grated rind of 1 small orange
10 ready-to-eat dried apricots, halved
6 ready-to-eat prunes, stoned and halved
20 g/³⁄₄ oz dried apple rings, halved
4 tbsp dried cranberries
2 tbsp coconut chips

1. Put the quinoa into a medium-sized saucepan with 225 ml/8 fl oz of the water. Add the honey, nutmeg and half the orange rind.

2. Bring to the boil, then cover and simmer over a very low heat for 10 minutes, or until most of the liquid has evaporated. Remove from the heat, but leave the pan covered for a further 7 minutes to allow the grains to swell. Fluff up with a fork.

3. Meanwhile, put the apricots, prunes, apple rings and cranberries into a separate saucepan. Add the remaining water and orange rind.

4. Bring to the boil, then simmer over a medium heat for 4–5 minutes, until the fruit is soft. Drain, reserving the liquid.

5. Divide the quinoa between two bowls. Spoon the fruit over the top and pour over the cooking liquid.

6. Sprinkle with the coconut chips and serve immediately.

TROPICAL SPIN
To give a more tropical taste, replace the dried prunes with dried pineapple.

PER SERVING: 414 KCALS | 4.6G FAT | 1.8G SAT FAT | 86.6G CARBS | 48.7G SUGARS | 9G FIBRE | 6.9G PROTEIN | TRACE SALT

APPLE AND SEED MUESLI

Know for sure that you are eating zero gluten content by combining these wholesome ingredients into a delicious and filling healthy breakfast muesli.

SERVES: 10
PREP: 15 MINS, PLUS COOLING COOK: 5 MINS

75 g/2³⁄₄ oz sunflower seeds
50 g/1³⁄₄ oz pumpkin seeds
90 g/3¹⁄₄ oz hazelnuts, roughly chopped
125 g/4¹⁄₂ oz buckwheat flakes
125 g/4¹⁄₂ oz rice flakes
125 g/4¹⁄₂ oz millet flakes
115 g/4 oz ready-to-eat dried apple, roughly chopped
115 g/4 oz ready-to-eat dried dates, stoned and roughly chopped

1. Place a frying pan over a medium heat. Add the sunflower seeds, pumpkin seeds and hazelnuts and toast, shaking the frying pan frequently for 4 minutes, or until they are golden brown.

2. Transfer the seed mixture to a large bowl and leave to cool.

3. Add the buckwheat flakes, rice flakes, millet flakes, dried apple and dates to the bowl and mix well.

4. Serve immediately or store in an airtight container for up to five days.

NUTRIENT POWERHOUSE
Buckwheat is a seed, although many people mistakenly think of it as a grain. It is a nutrition powerhouse, containing lots of protein. It is also a good source of fibre.

PER SERVING: 318 KCALS | 12.9G FAT | 1.5G SAT FAT | 45.8G CARBS | 14.2G SUGARS | 5.1G FIBRE | 9.2G PROTEIN | TRACE SALT

APPLE, CARROT AND CUCUMBER JUICE

Packed with nutrients and minerals, this fresh combination of ingredients is an effective way to kick-start your metabolism in the morning.

SERVES: 1
PREP: 5 MINS COOK: NONE

1 apple, unpeeled, cored
and chopped
1 carrot, peeled and chopped
½ cucumber, chopped

DECORATION
pieces of carrot, cucumber
and apple on a cocktail stick (optional)

1. Place the ingredients in a juicer or blender and process.

2. Pour into a glass. If using, put the pieces of carrot, cucumber and apple onto a cocktail stick and set on top of the glass. Serve.

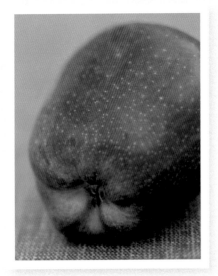

CUCUMBER COCKTAIL
Cucumbers provide a superb basis for a vegetable juice because of their high water content and mild flavour.

PER SERVING: 140 KCALS | 0.5G FAT | 0G SAT FAT | 24G CARBS | 24G SUGARS | 2G FIBRE | 2G PROTEIN | 0.1G SALT

PEAR, OAT AND BLUEBERRY BREAKFAST LOAF

Blueberries and pears are a powerful combination, with blueberries full of antioxidants and pears with significant fibre as well as vitamins C and K.

MAKES: 1
PREP: 30 MINS COOK: 55 MINS–1 HOUR

200 g/7 oz caster sugar
100 g/3½ oz butter, plus extra for greasing
2 large eggs, beaten
½ tsp vanilla essence
125 g/4½ oz gluten-free, wheat-free plain flour, sifted
1 tsp gluten-free baking powder
½ tsp gluten-free bicarbonate of soda
¼ tsp xanthan gum
85 g/3 oz gluten-free, wheat-free oats, plus extra for sprinkling
pinch of salt
½ tsp ground cinnamon
3 bananas, mashed
4 tbsp milk
2 cooked or canned pear halves, diced
70 g/2½ oz blueberries
10 g/¼ oz demerara sugar, for sprinkling

1. Preheat the oven to 180°C/350°F/Gas Mark 4. Grease a 900-g/2-lb loaf tin and line with baking paper.

2. Cream the sugar and butter in a bowl. Add the eggs and vanilla essence slowly.

3. In a separate bowl, mix together the flour, baking powder, bicarbonate of soda, xanthan gum, oats, salt and cinnamon and then add to the egg mixture. Add the mashed banana and milk and mix well until combined.

4. Spoon half of the mix into the prepared loaf tin and then sprinkle with the diced pear and two thirds of the blueberries. Spoon the remaining sponge mixture on top. Scatter over the remaining blueberries, the oats and the demerara sugar.

5. Bake in the preheated oven for 55 minutes–1 hour, or until a skewer inserted comes out clean. Remove from the oven and leave to cool in the tin.

NATURAL THICKENER
Xanthan gum is a natural product grown from the fermentation of the plant bacteria, xanthomonas campestris. It is used as a thickener to bind gluten-free bread and bakes.

PER LOAF: 2967 KCALS | 110G FAT | 61G SAT FAT | 44G CARBS | 284G SUGARS | 15G FIBRE | 40G PROTEIN | 6.7G SALT

APRICOT AND RAISIN OAT BARS

There's no need to stick to traditional breakfast formats – these oat bars, combining natural sugars and gluten-free oats, offer the perfect simple start to the day.

MAKES: 12
PREP: 25 MINS, PLUS COOLING   COOK: 45–50 MINS

350 g/12 oz ready-to-eat dried apricots
2 tbsp sunflower oil, plus extra for oiling
finely grated rind of ½ orange
seeds from 5 cardamom pods, crushed (optional)
140 g/5 oz raisins
115 g/4 oz gluten-free rolled oats

1. Put the apricots into a saucepan with enough water to cover. Cook over a medium heat until almost boiling, then reduce the heat and simmer for 5 minutes, or until completely soft. Drain.

2. Put the apricots into a food processor with the 2 tablespoons of oil and purée.

3. Tip the purée into a bowl and stir in the orange rind and the cardamom seeds, if using. Leave to cool.

4. Preheat the oven to 180°C/350°F/Gas Mark 4. Brush a 20-cm/8-inch square baking tin with oil.

5. Stir the raisins and oats into the apricot mixture. Spread out in the prepared tin, levelling the surface with a spatula.

6. Bake in the preheated oven for 35–40 minutes, until firm. Cover with foil after about 25 minutes to prevent burning.

7. Leave to cool in the tin for 15 minutes. Turn out onto a wire rack and leave to cool completely before cutting into the bars.

MORNING SUSTENANCE
The oats in this breakfast bar help to make this a filling start to the day.

PER SERVING: 162 KCALS | 3.1G FAT | 0.4G SAT FAT | 34.1G CARBS | 22.7G SUGARS | 3.6G FIBRE | 2.6G PROTEIN | TRACE SALT

COCONUT BREAKFAST COOKIES

A little preparation the previous evening, and these wheat and gluten-free cookies will provide a sustaining breakfast when time is against you.

MAKES: 6
PREP: 10–15 MINS COOK: 12–15 MINS

1 tbsp sunflower oil, for greasing
115 g/4 oz Brazil nuts
85 g/3 oz icing sugar
100 g/3½ oz buckwheat flour
½ tsp gluten-free baking powder
½ tsp xanthan gum
85 g/3 oz sultanas
25 g/1 oz desiccated coconut
2 egg whites
3 tsp poppy seeds, to sprinkle
3 tsp dark muscovado sugar, to sprinkle

1. Preheat the oven to 180°C/350°F/Gas Mark 4. Lightly grease a large baking sheet.

2. Place the Brazil nuts, icing sugar and buckwheat flour in a food processor and process until finely ground. Transfer the mixture to a large bowl then stir in the baking powder and xanthan gum.

3. Stir in the sultanas, coconut and egg whites, and combine thoroughly, using your hands, until a soft, sticky dough forms.

4. Divide the mixture into six and roll each piece into a ball. Place on the prepared baking sheet and press each ball with your fingers to create 12–cm/4½-inch rounds. Sprinkle lightly with poppy seeds and muscovado sugar.

5. Bake in the preheated oven for 12–15 minutes, or until firm and just beginning to brown. Leave to cool on the baking sheet before serving.

SOMETHING DIFFERENT

For a change of flavour, replace the sultanas with an equal amount of chopped dried apricots. and the Brazils with chopped blanched almonds.

PER SERVING: 345 KCALS | 17.8G FAT | 5.6G SAT FAT | 42G CARBS | 25G SUGARS | 4.7G FIBRE | 7.1G PROTEIN | 0.5G SALT

BLUEBERRY AND OATMEAL MUFFINS

Blueberries and muffins are a winning ingredient pairing, and when there's a gluten-free element, then the breakfast picture is complete.

MAKES: 9
PREP: 15 MINS COOK: 20–25 MINS

250 ml/9 fl oz pure orange juice
60 g/2¼ oz gluten-free, wheat-free porridge oats
100 g/3½ oz caster sugar
200 g/7 oz gluten-free, wheat-free plain flour, sifted
½ tsp xanthan gum
1½ tsp gluten-free baking powder
½ tsp gluten-free bicarbonate of soda
½ tsp cinnamon
¼ tsp mixed spice
125 ml/4 fl oz vegetable oil
1 egg, beaten
1 tsp glycerine
175 g/6 oz blueberries
1 tbsp demerara sugar, to sprinkle

1. Preheat the oven to 180°C/350°F/Gas 4. Line a 9-hole deep muffin tray with paper muffin cases.

2. Add the orange juice to the porridge oats and mix well in a bowl.

3. In a separate bowl, mix the sugar, flour, xanthan gum, baking powder, bicarbonate of soda and spices. Add the oil, egg and glycerine to the dry mixture and mix well. Then add the oat mixture and blueberries and fold these in gently.

4. Divide the mixture between the muffin cases and sprinkle with demerara sugar.

5. Bake the muffins in the preheated oven for 20–25 minutes or until a skewer comes out clean when inserted. Remove from the oven and cool on a wire rack.

MORNING DELIGHTS
Get your day off to a roaring start with these little balls of energy, and keep your conscience clear because the blueberries add extra nutritional value!

PER SERVING: 281 KCALS | 12G FAT | 1G SAT FAT | 39G CARBS | 17G SUGARS | 1.7G FIBRE | 10G PROTEIN | 0.4G SALT

EGGS IN PEPPER AND TOMATO SAUCE

This superbly healthy dish, using a selection of fresh, natural ingredients, provides as comforting a hot weekend brunch as you can imagine.

SERVES: 4
PREP: 20 MINS COOK: 30 MINS

4 large tomatoes
1½ tbsp rapeseed oil
1 large onion, finely chopped
½ tsp coriander seeds, crushed
½ tsp caraway seeds, crushed
2 red peppers, deseeded and roughly chopped
¼ tsp dried red chilli flakes
1 large garlic clove, thinly sliced
4 eggs
salt and pepper (optional)
1 tbsp roughly chopped fresh flat-leaf parsley, to garnish

1. Put the tomatoes in a shallow bowl and cover with boiling water. Leave for 30 seconds, then drain. Slip off the skins and discard, then chop the tomatoes.

2. Heat the oil in a large frying pan over a medium heat. Add the onion, coriander seeds and caraway seeds. Fry, stirring occasionally, for 10 minutes, or until the onion is soft and golden.

3. Stir in the red peppers and chilli flakes and fry for 5 minutes more, or until softened. Add the garlic and tomatoes and season with salt and pepper, if using. Reduce the heat to low and simmer, uncovered, for 10 minutes.

4. Crack the eggs over the surface. Cover and cook for a further 4–5 minutes, or until the eggs are cooked to your liking. Season with salt and pepper, if using, sprinkle with the parsley and serve immediately.

TOP TOMATOES
Tomatoes contain vitamins A, C and E, as well as zinc and selenium, all of which can help fight harmful free radicals.

PER SERVING: 189 KCALS | 11.2G FAT | 2.1G SAT FAT | 13.7G CARBS | 7.5G SUGARS | 3.8G FIBRE | 9.2G PROTEIN | 1.7G SALT

MUSHROOM RÖSTIS

This is truly satisfying breakfast fare. The röstis can also be prepared as a vegetarian main meal or as a snack served with yogurt or crème fraîche.

SERVES: 4
PREP: 25 MINS COOK: 20–25 MINS

300 g/10½ oz celeriac, peeled
1 small onion
3 tbsp chopped fresh parsley
4 portobello mushrooms (about 100 g/3½ oz)
4 tbsp olive oil
4 eggs
2 tbsp milk
salt and pepper (optional)

1. Preheat the oven to 200°C/400°F/Gas Mark 6. Coarsely grate the celeriac and onion in a food processor or by hand. Add 2 tablespoons of the parsley and season well.

2. Place the mushrooms on a baking sheet, brush with about 1 tablespoon of oil and season with salt and pepper, if using. Bake for 10–12 minutes.

3. Heat 2 tablespoons of the oil in a large, heavy-based frying pan. Place four large spoonfuls of the celeriac mixture in the pan, pressing with a palette knife to flatten. Fry for about 10 minutes, turning once, until golden. Drain on kitchen paper and keep hot.

4. Meanwhile, beat the eggs with the milk, remaining parsley and salt and pepper, if using. Heat the remaining oil in a small pan and cook the egg, stirring, until just set.

5. Place the röstis on warmed serving plates, top each with a mushroom and spoon over the scrambled eggs.

CELERIAC RECHARGE

Celeriac is low in calories and its flesh is full of healthy plant nutrients, minerals, vitamins and fibre. It is also a rich source of vitamin K.

PER SERVING: 218 KCALS | 17G FAT | 3G SAT FAT | 3.5G CARBS | 3G SUGARS | 5G FIBRE | 10G PROTEIN | 0.4G SALT

RED BEETROOT HASH

The perfect Saturday brunch, this dish contains antioxidant-rich sweet potatoes, low-carbohydrate Jerusalem artichokes and cholesterol-lowering beetroot.

SERVES: 4
PREP: 30 MINS COOK: 45 MINS

350 g/12 oz Jerusalem artichokes, unpeeled and scrubbed
450 g/1 lb raw beetroot, cut into cubes
750 g/1 lb 10 oz sweet potatoes, cut into cubes
2 tbsp olive oil
1 red onion, roughly chopped
2 tsp mild paprika
½ tsp mustard powder
3 tsp fresh thyme, plus extra to garnish
4 eggs
salt and pepper (optional)

1. Halve any of the larger artichokes. Half–fill the base of a steamer with water, bring to the boil, then add the artichokes to the water. Put the beetroot in one half of the steamer top, cover with a lid and steam for 10 minutes. Put the sweet potatoes in the other half of the top, so the colour of the beetroot won't bleed into the sweet potatoes.

2. Cover with a lid again and steam for 10 minutes more, or until all the vegetables are just tender. Drain the artichokes, peel them and cut them into cubes.

3. Heat 1 tablespoon of oil in a frying pan over a medium heat. Add the red onion and fry for 3–4 minutes, or until beginning to soften. Add the artichokes, beetroot and sweet potatoes and fry for 10 minutes, or until browned.

4. Stir in the paprika, mustard powder and thyme and season well with salt and pepper. Make four spaces in the frying pan, drizzle in the remaining oil, then crack an egg into each hole. Sprinkle the eggs with salt and pepper, if using, then cover and cook for 4–5 minutes, or until the eggs are cooked to your liking.

5. Spoon onto plates and serve immediately, garnished with extra thyme.

VEGETABLE DIGESTION
Knobbly–looking Jerusalem artichokes are considered to help digestion. What's more, they're packed with fibre, helping you to feel fuller for longer.

PER SERVING: 134 KCALS | 12.6G FAT | 2.7G SAT FAT | 68.1G CARBS | 26.1G SUGARS | 11.6G FIBRE | 14.2G PROTEIN | 1.4G SALT

BROCCOLI HASH

This version of hash features a mixture of healthy vegetables – broccoli, red pepper and potatoes – and a touch of chilli, creating a breakfast to remember.

SERVES: 4
PREP: 15 MINS COOK: 25 MINS

400 g/14 oz floury potatoes (e.g. Maris Piper)
cut into 1–cm/½–inch cubes
175 g/6 oz broccoli, cut into small florets
2 tbsp sunflower oil
1 onion, finely chopped
1 large red pepper, cut into small dice
¼–½ tsp dried chilli flakes
4 large eggs
salt and pepper (optional)

1. Cook the potatoes in lightly salted boiling water for 6 minutes. Drain well. Blanch or steam the broccoli for 3 minutes.

2. Heat the oil in a large frying pan over a fairly high heat, add the onion and red pepper and fry for 2–3 minutes to soften. Add the potatoes and cook, turning occasionally, for 6–8 minutes, until tender.

3. Stir in the broccoli and chilli flakes then leave over a low heat, turning the mixture occasionally until golden brown. Add salt and pepper to taste, if using.

4. Meanwhile, bring a wide pan of water to just simmering point. Break the eggs into the water and poach gently for 3–4 minutes, until softly set.

5. Spoon the hash onto warmed plates and top each portion with a poached egg.

BRILLIANT BROCCOLI
This versatile vegetable offers a rich supply of vitamins K and C, and is also a good source of folic acid, potassium and fibre.

PER SERVING: 275 KCALS | 12G FAT | 2.5G SAT FAT | 25G CARBS | 6G SUGARS | GG FIBRE | 13.5G PROTEIN | 0.3G SALT

LUNCHES AND SNACKS

SPICED CHICKPEA AND SPINACH SOUP

Here is a wholesome, gluten-free lunch. The chickpeas are a high-fibre source of complex carbs and protein, and the spinach can help protect your digestive system.

SERVES: 4
PREP: 20 MINS, PLUS CHILLING   COOK: 25 MINS

1 tbsp vegetable oil
1 onion, finely chopped
2 garlic cloves, crushed
1 tsp cumin seeds
2 tsp medium curry powder
1 tsp hot chilli powder
400 g/14 oz canned chickpeas, drained and rinsed
400 g/14 oz canned chopped tomatoes
500 ml/17 fl oz gluten-free vegetable stock
100 g/3½ oz spinach, de-stalked and chopped
salt and pepper (optional)

MINT DRESSING
100 g/3½ oz natural yogurt
2 tbsp finely chopped fresh mint leaves
salt and pepper (optional)

1. Heat the oil in a saucepan over a medium heat. Add the onion and sauté for 4–5 minutes, or until starting to soften.

2. Add the garlic, cumin seeds, curry and chilli powders and cook for 1 minute, stirring constantly.

3. Add the chickpeas, tomatoes and stock and season to taste with salt and pepper, if using. Bring to the boil, then reduce the heat, cover and simmer for 15 minutes.

4. Meanwhile, to make the mint dressing, mix the yogurt and mint together and season to taste with salt and pepper, if using. Cover and chill until ready to serve.

5. Stir the spinach into the soup and cook for a further 1–2 minutes, or until the spinach has wilted. Serve with a little of the mint dressing drizzled over.

DID YOU KNOW?
Although spinach is rich in calcium, our bodies are unable to absorb most of it due to the oxalates in the leaves that inhibit this. However, these oxalates don't appear to adversely affect iron absorption.

PER SERVING: 189 KCALS | 6.5G FAT | 1G SAT FAT | 20G CARBS | 8.5G SUGARS | 7G FIBRE | 9G PROTEIN | 0.3G SALT

CRAB AND GINGER SOUP

You'll remember this delicious soup for its balance of addictive flavours and enticing aromas. It's an excellent dish for impressing friends and for special occasion dining.

SERVES: 4
PREP: 20 MINS COOK: 35 MINS

2 tbsp chilli oil
1 garlic clove, chopped
4 spring onions, trimmed and sliced
2 red peppers, deseeded and chopped
1 tbsp grated fresh ginger
1 litre/1¾ pints gluten-free fish stock
100 ml/3½ fl oz coconut milk
100 ml/3½ fl oz rice wine
2 tbsp lime juice
1 tbsp grated lime rind
6 young kaffir lime leaves, finely shredded
300 g/10½ oz freshly cooked crabmeat
200 g/7 oz freshly cooked crab claws
150 g/5½ oz canned sweetcorn, drained
1 tbsp chopped fresh coriander, plus a few sprigs to garnish
salt and pepper (optional)

1. Heat the oil in a large saucepan. Add the garlic and spring onions and cook, stirring for about 3 minutes, until slightly softened. Add the peppers and ginger and cook for a further 4 minutes, stirring.

2. Pour in the stock and season with salt and pepper, if using. Bring to the boil, then reduce the heat.

3. Pour in the coconut milk, rice wine and lime juice, and stir in the grated lime rind and kaffir lime leaves. Leave to simmer for 15 minutes.

4. Add the crabmeat and crab claws to the soup with the corn and coriander. Cook for 5 minutes, or until the crab is heated through.

5. Ladle into warmed soup bowls, garnish with coriander and serve immediately.

MAGICAL COMBINATION
This delicious Thai-inspired soup contains sweet coconut milk which is offset perfectly by the aromatic ginger and zingy lime juice.

PER SERVING: 305 KCALS | 15.5G FAT | 7.1G SAT FAT | 15.4G CARBS | 3G SUGARS | 3.1G FIBRE | 25.4G PROTEIN | 6G SALT

THREE-BEAN
ENERGY-BOOSTER SALAD

This mighty salad will give you a slow, sustained energy boost. It is made with low-GI foods that are rich in fibre and carbohydrate.

SERVES: 4
PREP: 20 MINS COOK: 8–10 MINS

200 g/7 oz green beans, halved
200 g/7 oz frozen edamame beans
or frozen broad beans
150 g/5½ oz frozen sweetcorn
400 g/14 oz canned red kidney beans,
drained and rinsed
2 tbsp chia seeds

DRESSING
3 tbsp olive oil
1 tbsp red wine vinegar
1 tsp wholegrain mustard
1 tsp agave syrup
4 tsp finely chopped fresh tarragon
salt and pepper (optional)

1. Put the green beans, edamame beans and sweetcorn in a saucepan of boiling water. Bring back to the boil, then simmer for 4 minutes, until the green beans are just tender. Drain into a colander, rinse with cold water, then drain again and put into a salad bowl.

2. Add the kidney beans and chia seeds to the bowl and toss gently together.

3. To make the dressing, put the oil, vinegar and mustard in a jam jar, then add the agave syrup and tarragon and season to taste with salt and pepper, if using. Screw on the lid and shake well. Drizzle over the salad, toss gently together and serve immediately.

THREE CHEERS FOR CHIA
Originally eaten by the Mayans and Aztecs, chia seeds are rich in protein, which helps to build and repair muscles. They are the richest combined plant source of omega–3, –6 and –9 fatty acids. A tablespoon of chia seeds provides 5 g of fibre; women should aim for 25 g of fibre per day and a man 38 g.

PER SERVING: 312 KCALS | 14.5G FAT | 2G SAT FAT | 26G CARBS | 6.5G SUGARS | 13G FIBRE | 13.5G PROTEIN | 0.1G SALT

TURKEY, RICE AND CRANBERRY SALAD

Here's how to enjoy the flavour of turkey in a salad. You could take this to a bring-and-share supper, or pack individual portions for a work lunch.

SERVES: 4
PREP: 25 MINS, PLUS COOLING COOK: 30 MINS

150 g/5½ oz brown basmati rice
40 g/1½ oz wild rice
250 g/9 oz raw turkey breast slices
40 g/1½ oz dried cranberries
3 spring onions, finely chopped
200 g/7 oz tomatoes, diced
1 small red pepper, halved, deseeded and cut into chunks
55 g/2 oz rocket
40 g/1½ oz wafer-thin sliced lean ready-to-eat ham, cut into strips
salt and pepper (optional)

DRESSING

1½ tbsp cranberry sauce
1½ tbsp sherry vinegar
finely grated rind and juice of 1 small lemon
1 tbsp Dijon mustard

1. Put cold water in the base of a steamer, bring to the boil, then add the brown rice and wild rice and bring back to the boil. Put the turkey in the top of the steamer in a single layer, season with salt and pepper, if using, then put it on the steamer base, cover and steam for 15 minutes, or until the turkey is cooked; cut into the middle of a slice to check that the meat is no longer pink and that the juices are clear and piping hot. Remove the steamer top and cook the rice for 5—10 minutes more, or until tender.

2. Dice the turkey and put it in a bowl. Add the cranberries. Drain and rinse the rice, then add to the bowl.

3. To make the dressing, put the cranberry sauce in a small saucepan and place over a low heat until just melted. Remove from the heat, then add the vinegar, lemon rind and juice, mustard and a little salt and pepper, if using. Whisk together until smooth, then drizzle over the salad and leave to cool.

4. Add the spring onions, tomatoes and red pepper to the salad. Toss gently together, then divide between four plates. Top with the rocket and ham and serve.

DID YOU KNOW?

Meat from turkeys that graze on natural pasture contains a little more fat, including some omega-3 fats, and more carotenes than meat from penned turkeys.

PER SERVING: 320 KCALS | 3G FAT | 0.7G SAT FAT | 48G CARBS | 12.5G SUGARS | 4G FIBRE | 23G PROTEIN | 0.6G SALT

WARM CHICKEN AND MANGO SALAD

The combination of chicken and mango takes many main course forms. This salad has an invigorating sweetness, which derives from the mango and the honey.

SERVES: 4
PREP: 25 MINS COOK: 12 MINS

1 tbsp groundnut oil
600 g/1 lb 5 oz chicken breasts,
skinned and cut into strips
280 g/10 oz French beans, topped and tailed
and cut into 2.5-cm/1-inch lengths
280 g/10 oz Chinese leaves, finely shredded
4 tbsp chopped fresh coriander
85 g/3 oz roasted salted peanuts, finely chopped
1 mango, peeled, stoned and diced

DRESSING
2 tbsp Thai fish sauce
1 tbsp clear honey
4 tbsp lemon juice
1 red chilli, deseeded and finely chopped

1. Heat the oil in a preheated wok or large frying pan until smoking. Add the chicken strips and stir-fry for 2 minutes to seal. Add the beans, reduce the heat, cover and cook for a further 5 minutes, stirring halfway through to prevent burning. Keep warm by covering with a lid.

2. Meanwhile, prepare the dressing by mixing all the ingredients together in a small bowl. Set aside.

3. Toss together the Chinese leaves, coriander and peanuts in a large serving bowl.

4. Add the mango, chicken and beans to the serving bowl, then pour over the dressing. Toss to coat and serve immediately.

MANGO BOOST
Eating mangoes is believed to improve digestion and bone health, decrease the risk of colon cancer, and to benefit the skin and hair.

PER SERVING: 436 KCALS | 18.5G FAT | 3G SAT FAT | 31G CARBS | 21.2G SUGARS | 6.2G FIBRE | 40.5G PROTEIN | 2.4G SALT

REFRESHING SEARED BEEF SALAD

A Thai-inspired salad with wafer-thin, sliced and seared steak, peppery radishes, nutrient-boosting kale, mint and coriander, all drizzled with a zesty lime dressing.

SERVES: 4

PREP: 20–25 MINS COOK: 6–10 MINS, PLUS RESTING

½ iceberg lettuce, leaves separated and torn into bite–sized pieces
200 g/7 oz radishes, thinly sliced
4 shallots, thinly sliced
85 g/3 oz kale, shredded
2 tbsp dried goji berries
25 g/1 oz fresh mint, roughly chopped
25 g/1 oz fresh coriander, roughly chopped
2 x 250 g/9 oz sirloin steaks, visible fat removed
4 tbsp sunflower oil
juice of 1 lime
1 tbsp gluten–free soy sauce
salt and pepper (optional)

1. Put the lettuce, radishes and shallots in a serving bowl. Sprinkle over the kale, goji berries, mint and coriander, then toss gently together.

2. Preheat a ridged griddle pan over a high heat. Brush the steaks with 1 tablespoon of oil, then sprinkle with a little salt and pepper, if using. Cook in the hot pan for 2 minutes on each side for medium–rare, 3 minutes for medium or 4 minutes for well done. Transfer the steaks to a plate and leave to rest for a few minutes.

3. Meanwhile, to make the dressing, put the lime juice, soy sauce and remaining 3 tablespoons of oil in a jam jar, screw on the lid and shake well. Drizzle over the salad, then toss together.

4. Divide the salad between four bowls. Thinly slice the steak and arrange it over the top, then serve immediately.

MINT FOR YOUR TUMMY

Fresh mint leaves freshen the palate and are rich in chlorophyll, antioxidants and the essential oils menthol, menthione and menthol acetate. Mint is thought to help relieve symptoms of irritable bowel syndrome by relieving bloating and abdominal discomfort.

PER SERVING: 358 KCALS | 20G FAT | 3.6G SAT FAT | 13.3G CARBS | 6.7G SUGARS | 4G FIBRE | 31.3G PROTEIN | 1.7G SALT

CHICKEN AND AVOCADO TACOS

The introduction of gluten-free tacos has brought the goodness and softness of a great tasting tortilla to those avoiding gluten – in all other respects this is a classic.

SERVES: 4
PREP: 20–25 MINS COOK: 10–13 MINS

1 ripe avocado
150 ml/5 fl oz natural yogurt
2 tbsp medium cornmeal
1 tsp chilli powder
½ tsp dried thyme
600 g/1 lb 5 oz skinless chicken breasts,
cut into thin strips
2 tbsp sunflower oil
1 red onion, sliced
1 large red pepper, deseeded and sliced
1 large green pepper, deseeded and sliced
8 gluten-free taco shells
salt and pepper (optional)
½ tsp smoked paprika, to garnish

1. Halve the avocado, remove the stone and scoop out the flesh, then purée in a blender with the yogurt. Season to taste with salt and pepper, if using.

2. Mix together the cornmeal, chilli and thyme with salt and pepper, if using, to taste in a large bowl. Add the chicken and toss to coat evenly.

3. Heat the oil in a wok or large frying pan and stir-fry the onion and peppers for 3–4 minutes to soften. Remove and keep hot.

4. Add the chicken and stir-fry for 5–6 minutes, until evenly browned. Return the vegetables to the pan and stir-fry for a further 1–2 minutes.

5. Spoon the chicken mixture into the taco shells and top with a spoonful of the avocado mixture. Sprinkle with smoked paprika and serve.

DID YOU KNOW?

Chicken is a good source of vitamin B6 and phosphorus, and of protein, niacin and selenium.

PER SERVING: 502 KCALS | 22.5G FAT | 3.5G SAT FAT | 30G CARBS | 9G SUGARS | 5.5G FIBRE | 42.5G PROTEIN | 0.4G SALT

SPICED GRAM FLOUR ROLLS

Making these delicate, lightly spiced gram flour rolls is almost like making an Indian-style pasta. Creating perfect-looking rolls may take a bit of practice!

MAKES: 24

PREP: 30–35 MINS, PLUS STANDING COOK: 30 MINS

1 tbsp vegetable or groundnut oil, for oiling
250 g/9 oz gram flour, sifted
100 g/3½ oz set natural yogurt
600 ml/1 pint warm water
2 tsp salt
¼ tsp ground turmeric
2 tsp grated fresh ginger
2 garlic cloves, crushed
4 tsp green chilli paste

TOPPING

6 tbsp vegetable or groundnut oil
1 tsp sesame seeds
1 tsp black mustard seeds
4 tbsp finely chopped fresh coriander
2 tbsp freshly grated coconut

1. Lightly brush four large baking trays with oil and set aside.

2. Place the gram flour, yogurt and water in a heavy-based saucepan with the salt, turmeric, ginger, garlic and chilli paste. Whisk until smooth, then place over a medium heat and continue to whisk constantly. When the batter starts to thicken (after about 5–6 minutes), reduce the heat to low, cover and cook for 4–5 minutes. Stir, re-cover and cook for a further 2–3 minutes, or until thickened and smooth.

3. Remove from the heat and ladle the batter onto the prepared baking trays, using a palette knife to spread the mixture as thinly as possible. The batter will start to set as it cools. Leave to stand for 5 minutes, then slice it lengthways into 5-cm/2-inch wide strips. This quantity should make about 24 rolls.

4. Starting at one end of each strip, use the palette knife to gently lift and roll (like a small Swiss roll). Repeat until all the strips have been rolled. Transfer to a serving plate.

5. Meanwhile, make the topping. Heat the oil in a frying pan and add the sesame seeds and mustard seeds. When the seeds start to pop, remove from the heat and drizzle the spiced oil over the gram-flour rolls. Sprinkle over the coriander and coconut. Serve warm or at room temperature.

PER SERVING: 79 KCALS | 4.5G FAT | 0.8G SAT FAT | 6G CARBS | 0.6G SUGARS | 1G FIBRE | 3G PROTEIN | 0.4G SALT

POLENTA BRUSCHETTAS
WITH TAPENADE

Polenta bruschettas are a real gluten-free treat and this combination of tomatoes, olives and capers is just one example of a tasty bruschetta topping.

SERVES: 4

PREP: 25 MINS, PLUS SETTING   COOK: 15–20 MINS

500 ml/17 fl oz boiling water
pinch of salt
100 g/3½ oz quick–cook polenta
2 tbsp olive oil, plus extra for greasing
16 cherry vine tomatoes
salt and pepper (optional)

TAPENADE
25 g/1 oz sun–dried tomatoes
55 g/2 oz pitted black olives
2 tbsp salted capers, rinsed
2 tbsp chopped fresh flat–leaf parsley
1 garlic clove, crushed
juice of ½ lemon
2 tbsp extra virgin olive oil

1. Place the water in a saucepan with a pinch of salt and bring to the boil. Sprinkle in the polenta and stir over a medium heat for about 5 minutes, or until thick and smooth.

2. Grease a 450 g/1 lb loaf tin. Stir the oil into the polenta mix, add salt and pepper to taste, if using, and then spread the mixture into the prepared tin. Leave to set.

3. To make the tapenade, finely chop the sun–dried tomatoes, olives, capers and parsley. Mix with the garlic, lemon juice and oil, and add salt and pepper to taste, if using.

4. Preheat the grill to high. Cut the polenta into eight slices and arrange on a baking sheet with the tomatoes. Brush the polenta with oil and grill until golden, turning once.

5. Serve the polenta slices topped with a spoonful of tapenade and the tomatoes.

PREPARED POLENTA
If you'd rather not make your own polenta, you can buy it ready made in the Italian, ethnic or refrigerated section of your grocery store.

PER SERVING: 266 KCALS | 15.4G FAT | 2.1G SAT FAT | 28.4G CARBS | 5.1G SUGARS | 4.2G FIBRE | 4.3G PROTEIN | 1.6G SALT

MONKFISH CEVICHE WITH RED QUINOA

Ceviche has its origins in Persia, and continues to be regarded as a special treat. Monkfish works well here, but it can be replaced with any other firm white fish.

SERVES: 4
PREP: 25 MINS, PLUS MARINATING
COOK: 20 MINS, PLUS STANDING

450 g/1 lb monkfish fillets
or other firm white fish, cubed
juice of 5–6 limes
60 g/2¼ oz red quinoa, rinsed
150 ml/5 fl oz water
4 tomatoes
1 red onion, diced
1–2 small fresh green jalapeño chillies,
deseeded and diced
4 tbsp chopped fresh coriander
1 large, ripe avocado, peeled, stoned and cubed
extra virgin olive oil, for drizzling
salt and pepper (optional)
lime wedges from half a lime, to garnish

1. Put the fish into a shallow, non–metallic dish. Pour over enough of the lime juice to cover and marinate in the refrigerator for 3 hours, stirring occasionally, until opaque. Drain the fish, discarding the juice.

2. Put the quinoa into a saucepan with the water. Bring to the boil, then reduce the heat, cover and simmer for 15 minutes. Remove from the heat, but leave the pan covered for a further 5 minutes to allow the grains to swell. Fluff up with a fork and set aside.

3. Halve the tomatoes and discard the seeds. Cut into small dice, and put into a bowl with the onion, chillies and coriander. Stir in the remaining lime juice. Add salt and pepper to taste, if using.

4. Divide the tomato mixture between four plates. Top with the fish and 2 tablespoons of the quinoa. (Reserve the remainder for use in another dish.) Scatter over the avocado.

5. Sprinkle with salt, if using, and drizzle with oil. Garnish with lime wedges and serve immediately.

QUINOA CHOICES
You can buy quinoa in red, white or black grains. It is botanically related to beetroot and spinach, and trumps the nutritional content of all other grains.

PER SERVING: 330 KCALS | 17G FAT | 2.5G SAT FAT | 26.2G CARBS | 5.1G SUGARS | 6.7G FIBRE | 21.1G PROTEIN | 1.6G SALT

GRILLED PRAWNS WITH CRISP-FRIED RED RICE

Looking for an easy-to-make lunch to restore and revitalize? This rice and prawn combination scores on both flavour and colour.

SERVES: 10
PREP: 35 MINS, PLUS MARINATING AND DRYING
COOK: 50 MINS

500 g/1 lb 2 oz raw tiger prawns, peeled and deveined
juice of 4 limes
1 small fresh red chilli, deseeded and finely chopped
5 tbsp olive oil
125 g/4½ oz Camargue red rice, rinsed
300 ml/10 fl oz water
½ tsp of salt
3 heads of red chicory, leaves separated
10–12 radishes, sliced
3 spring onions, sliced
4 tbsp red quinoa sprouts
salt and pepper (optional)

1. Put the prawns into a shallow dish. Stir in the lime juice, chilli and 2 tablespoons of the oil. Leave to marinate in the refrigerator for 2 hours.

2. Put the rice into a saucepan with the water and ½ teaspoon of salt. Bring to the boil, then cover and simmer for 40 minutes. Fluff up with a fork and spread on a tray to dry.

3. Meanwhile, soak four wooden skewers in a shallow dish of water for at least 30 minutes. Preheat the grill.

4. Tip the rice into a frying pan large enough to spread it out in a thin layer. Place over a medium–high heat and drizzle over the remaining oil. Fry for a few minutes until a crust forms. Turn and fry for a further few minutes. Keep warm over a low heat until ready to serve.

5. Meanwhile, drain the prawns, thread onto the soaked skewers and season to taste with salt and pepper, if using. Place under the preheated grill and cook for 5–6 minutes, until pink all over.

6. Divide the chicory between four plates and top with the rice, radishes and spring onions.

7. Remove the prawns from the skewers and arrange on top of the salad. Sprinkle with the quinoa sprouts and serve immediately.

PER SERVING: 142 KCALS | 6.5G FAT | 1G SAT FAT | 11G CARBS | 0.8G SUGARS | 1G FIBRE | 10G PROTEIN | 0.5G SALT

EASY VEGETABLE SUSHI

This vegetable sushi roll – made with creamy avocado, crunchy cucumber and matchsticks of red pepper – provides an economical and healthy speciality dish.

SERVES: 4
PREP: 30–35 MINS, PLUS COOLING AND CHILLING
COOK: 25 MINS

200 g/7 oz sushi rice
2–3 tbsp Japanese rice vinegar
pinch of salt
1 tbsp Japanese sweet rice wine (mirin)
7 sheets Japanese sushi nori, pretoasted
½ cucumber, cut into matchsticks
1 red pepper, deseeded and cut into matchsticks
1 avocado, cut into matchsticks
4 spring onions, halved lengthwise
gluten-free tamari, wasabi and sliced ginger, to serve (optional)

1. Place the rice in a saucepan and cover with 375 ml/13 fl oz of water. Bring to the boil, then reduce the heat to low, cover and simmer for 20 minutes. Drain the rice and transfer to a large bowl. Gently fold in the rice vinegar, salt and mirin and leave to cool.

2. When the rice is cold, place one sheet of pretoasted nori onto a sushi rolling mat, shiny side down, and spread a thin layer of rice all over, leaving a 1–cm/½-inch border along the far edge. Add a selection of the vegetable pieces, arranged in lines running the same way as the bamboo of the mat.

3. Use the mat to carefully lift the edge of the nori closest to you, roll it away from you and tuck it in as tightly as you can. Continue to roll up the nori tightly and, if necessary, moisten the far edge with a little water to seal the roll together. Repeat with the remaining nori sheets, rice and vegetables. Chill the rolls in the refrigerator, wrapped tightly in clingfilm, until required.

4. To serve, cut each roll into slices about 2.5 cm/1 inch thick. Serve with tamari and wasabi for dipping and sliced ginger as an accompaniment, if using.

A LIGHT LUNCH
This vegetarian dish makes a great light lunch and the wasabi adds a spicy kick!

PER SERVING: 278 KCALS | 5.9G FAT | 0.8G SAT FAT | 50.5G CARBS | 4.4G SUGARS | 6.9G FIBRE | 6.7G PROTEIN | 0.8G SALT

SALSA BEAN AND TOMATO DIP

The health benefits of aduki beans include improved digestion and increased energy levels. Their sweet, nutty flavour has a significant role in this flavoursome dip.

SERVES: 4
PREP: 20–25 MINS, PLUS CHILLING AND COOLING
COOK: 5–10 MINS

200 g/7 oz cherry tomatoes, quartered
1 small red onion, very finely chopped
200 g/7 oz canned aduki beans, drained and rinsed
½ red pepper, deseeded and finely chopped
½ or 1 red chilli, deseeded and very finely chopped
2 tsp sun-dried tomato purée
1 tsp agave nectar
large handful of chopped fresh coriander
salt and pepper (optional)

1. Place the tomatoes, onion, beans, red pepper, chilli, tomato purée, agave nectar and coriander in a large bowl. Mix together well and season to taste with salt and pepper, if using.

2. Cover the bowl and leave in the refrigerator for at least 15 minutes to let the flavours develop. Preheat the grill to medium.

3. Place the tortillas under the preheated grill and lightly toast. Leave to cool slightly then cut into slices.

4. Transfer the bean dip to a small bowl and serve.

TEMPTING TORTILLAS
Serve the bean dip with sliced tortillas and chilli oil for dipping.

PER SERVING: 80 KCALS | 1.1G FAT | 0.3G SAT FAT | 14G CARBS | 5.1G SUGARS | 3G FIBRE | 3.5G PROTEIN | 1.5G SALT

MAINS

Quinoa and beetroot burgers	74
Buckwheat, mushrooms and roasted squash	76
Pumpkin and chestnut risotto	78
Spiced parsnip gratin with ginger cream	80
Creole turkey-stuffed peppers	82
Baked sea bass with white bean purée	84
Prawn jambalaya	86
Pan-cooked roast chicken	88
Mexican chicken with rice	90
Chicken cannellini chilli	92
Barbecue-glazed spare ribs	94
Meatballs with tomato sauce	96
Roast pork with gingered apples	98

QUINOA AND BEETROOT BURGERS

Here's a burger with a difference. It will bring a resonant shade of purple to your plate, but in true burger tradition it still provides a tasty treat.

MAKES: 8
PREP: 35 MINS COOK: 1 HOUR 10 MINS

3–4 small beetroots, peeled and cubed, about 225 g/8 oz in total
135 g/4¾ oz quinoa, rinsed
350 ml/12 fl oz vegetable stock
½ small onion, grated
finely grated rind of ½ lemon
2 tsp cumin seeds
½ tsp salt
¼ tsp pepper
1 large egg white, lightly beaten
10 g/¼ oz quinoa flour, for dusting
1 tbsp vegetable oil, for shallow-frying
8 slices of sourdough toast, to serve
150 g/5½ oz peppery green salad leaves, to serve

WASABI BUTTER

1½ tsp wasabi powder
¾ tsp warm water
70 g/2½ oz butter, at room temperature

1. Cook the beetroots in a steamer for 1 hour.

2. Meanwhile, put the quinoa into a saucepan with the stock. Bring to the boil, then cover and simmer over a very low heat for 10 minutes. Remove from the heat, but leave the pan covered for a further 10 minutes to allow the grains to swell. Fluff up with a fork and spread out on a tray to dry.

3. To make the wasabi butter, mix together the wasabi powder and water. Mix with the butter and chill in the refrigerator.

4. Place the beetroots in a food processor and process until smooth. Tip into a bowl and mix with the quinoa, onion, lemon rind, cumin seeds, salt, pepper and egg white.

5. Divide the mixture into eight equal-sized portions and shape into burgers, each 15 mm/ ⅝ inch thick, firmly pressing the mixture together. Lightly dust with quinoa flour.

6. Heat a thin layer of oil in a non-stick frying pan. Add the burgers and fry over a medium-high heat, in batches if necessary, for 2 minutes on each side, turning carefully.

7. Place the burgers on the toast and serve with the wasabi butter and salad leaves.

PER SERVING: 281 KCALS | 11G FAT | 5G SAT FAT | 35G CARBS | 5G SUGARS | 4G FIBRE | 9G PROTEIN | 1.3G SALT

BUCKWHEAT, MUSHROOMS AND ROASTED SQUASH

Roasted buckwheat combined with mushrooms, onions and balsamic-glazed squash provides this dish with appetizingly rich flavours.

SERVES: 4
PREP: 25 MINS COOK: 30 MINS

1 kg/2 lb 4 oz squash, such as Crown Prince or Kabocha
1 tbsp gluten-free thick balsamic vinegar
125 ml/4 fl oz olive oil
large knob of butter
225 g/8 oz roasted buckwheat, rinsed
1 egg, lightly beaten
450 ml/15 fl oz hot gluten-free vegetable stock
½ teaspoon of salt
1 onion, halved and sliced
250 g/9 oz small chestnut mushrooms, quartered
2 tbsp lemon juice
6 tbsp chopped fresh flat-leaf parsley
25 g/1 oz walnut halves roughly chopped
additional salt and pepper (optional)

1. Preheat the oven to 200°C/400°F/Gas Mark 6. Cut the squash into eight wedges, peel and deseed.

2. Put the squash into a roasting tin and toss with the vinegar and 6 tablespoons of the oil. Season well with salt and pepper, if using, and dot with the butter. Roast in the preheated oven for 25–30 minutes, until slightly caramelised.

3. Meanwhile, put the buckwheat into a frying pan. Add the egg, stirring to coat the grains. Stir over a medium heat for 3 minutes, until the egg moisture has evaporated. Add the stock and ½ teaspoon of salt. Simmer for 9–10 minutes, until the grains are tender but not disintegrating. Remove from the heat.

4. Heat the remaining oil in a deep frying pan. Add the onion and fry over a medium heat for 10 minutes. Season to taste with salt and pepper, if using. Add the mushrooms and fry for 5 minutes. Stir in the buckwheat, lemon juice and most of the parsley.

5. Transfer the buckwheat mixture to four plates and arrange the squash on top. Scatter over the walnuts and the remaining parsley. Serve.

PER SERVING: 655 KCALS | 33G FAT | 6G SAT FAT | 70G CARBS | 15G SUGARS | 10G FIBRE | 13.5G PROTEIN | 0.9G SALT

PUMPKIN AND CHESTNUT RISOTTO

This comforting dish is full of nutritious content – pumpkin has vital antioxidants and vitamins, and chestnuts offer minerals, vitamins and phyto-nutrients.

SERVES: 4
PREP: 25 MINS COOK: 35 MINS

1 tbsp olive oil
40 g/1½ oz butter
1 small onion, finely chopped
225 g/8 oz pumpkin, diced
225 g/8 oz chestnuts, cooked and shelled
280 g/10 oz risotto rice
150 ml/5 fl oz gluten–free dry white wine
1 tsp crumbled saffron threads (optional),
dissolved in 4 tbsp of the stock
1 litre/1¾ pints simmering gluten–free vegetable stock
85 g/3 oz Parmesan cheese, freshly grated,
plus extra for serving
salt and pepper (optional)

1. Heat the oil with 25 g/1 oz of the butter in a deep saucepan over a medium heat until the butter has melted. Stir in the onion and pumpkin and cook, stirring occasionally, for 5 minutes, or until the onion is soft and starting to turn golden and the pumpkin begins to colour.

2. Roughly chop the chestnuts and add to the mixture. Stir thoroughly to coat.

3. Reduce the heat, add the rice and mix to coat in oil and butter. Cook, stirring constantly, for 2–3 minutes, or until the grains are translucent. Add the wine and cook, stirring constantly, for 1 minute, until the wine has reduced.

4. Add the saffron liquid to the rice, if using, and cook, stirring constantly, until the liquid has been absorbed.

5. Gradually add the simmering stock, a ladleful at a time, stirring constantly. Add more liquid as the rice absorbs each addition. Increase the heat to medium so that the liquid bubbles.

6. Cook for 20 minutes, or until all the liquid has been absorbed and the rice is creamy. Season to taste with salt and pepper, if using.

7. Remove the risotto from the heat and add the remaining butter. Mix well, then stir in the Parmesan until it melts. Adjust the seasoning if necessary.

8. Spoon the risotto onto four warmed plates, sprinkle with grated Parmesan and serve immediately.

PER SERVING: 602 KCALS | 20G FAT | 10G SAT FAT | 81G CARBS | 8G SUGARS | 5.4G FIBRE | 15.5G PROTEIN | 2.1G SALT

SPICED PARSNIP GRATIN WITH GINGER CREAM

Can you imagine a gratin with no potatoes? Well, here it is – earthy, sweet parsnips are the key ingredient, providing an inventive spin on the classic gratin.

SERVES: 6 PREP: 20 MINS
COOK: 45–50 MINS

butter, for greasing
3 large parsnips, approx
750 g/1 lb 10 oz, thinly sliced
425 ml/15 fl oz double cream
250 ml/9 fl oz gluten-free vegetable stock
1 garlic clove, crushed
2.5-cm/1-inch piece fresh ginger, roughly chopped and crushed in a garlic press
1/4 tsp white pepper
1/8 tsp freshly grated nutmeg, plus extra to garnish
sea salt (optional)
snipped fresh chives, to garnish

1. Lightly grease a large gratin dish. Place the parsnips in a steamer set over a saucepan of boiling water. Steam for 3 minutes, until barely tender, shaking halfway through cooking. Tip into the prepared dish and lightly season with salt, if using.

2. Preheat the oven to 180°C/350°F/Gas Mark 4. Gently heat the cream and stock in a saucepan with the garlic and ginger. Do not allow the mixture to boil. Add the pepper, nutmeg and sea salt, if using, to taste.

3. Pour the hot cream mixture over the parsnips. Cover the dish with foil and bake in the preheated oven for 20 minutes, with an oven tray underneath to catch any drips.

4. Remove the foil and bake for a further 15–20 minutes, until golden on top.

5. Sprinkle with a little more nutmeg and some chives and serve.

DID YOU KNOW?

Parsnips are related to carrots and are ideal to grow over the winter, when frosts give the root a superior flavour. In Roman times parsnips were thought to be an aphrodisiac.

PER SERVING: 456 KCALS | 40G FAT | 24G SAT FAT | 1G CARBS | 8G SUGARS | 6G FIBRE | 3.3G PROTEIN | 0.3G SALT

CREOLE TURKEY-STUFFED PEPPERS

Imagine these stuffed peppers as explosive bombs of flavour and you have an idea of the impact they can make on your dinner table.

SERVES: 4
PREP: 25 MINS COOK: 50–55 MINS

4 large red peppers, about 200 g/7 oz each
1 tbsp sunflower oil, plus extra for greasing
40 g/1½ oz gluten-free chorizo, skinned and diced
300 g/10½ oz fresh turkey mince
1 celery stick, finely chopped
1 onion, finely chopped
1 small green pepper, deseeded and finely chopped
100 g/3½ oz long-grain, easy-cook rice
200 ml/7 fl oz gluten-free vegetable stock
4 tbsp passata
2 tbsp chopped fresh parsley or snipped chives
½ tsp gluten-free hot pepper sauce, plus extra to serve
salt and pepper (optional)
salad leaves, to serve (optional)

1. Preheat the oven to 220°C/425°F/Gas Mark 7 and grease a baking dish. Cut off the red pepper tops and remove the cores and seeds, then set the peppers and tops aside.

2. Heat the oil in a frying pan over a medium heat. Add the chorizo and fry for 1–2 minutes until it gives off its oil. Transfer to a dish using a slotted spoon and set aside.

3. Pour off all but 2 tablespoons of oil from the pan. Add the turkey, celery, onion and green pepper and fry, stirring with a wooden spoon to break up the turkey into large clumps, for 3–5 minutes until the onion is soft. Stir in the rice.

4. Add the stock, passata, parsley and hot pepper sauce, and season to taste with salt and pepper, if using. Bring to the boil, stirring. Divide the mixture between the red peppers, then arrange them in the prepared dish, topped with their 'lids'. Carefully pour in boiling water to fill the dish up to 2.5 cm/1 inch, then cover tightly with foil.

5. Bake in the preheated oven for 40–45 minutes, or until the peppers are tender. Serve hot or at room temperature, with salad leaves and the chorizo.

PER SERVING: 382 KCALS | 17.7G FAT | 4.6G SAT FAT | 36.4G CARBS | 10G SUGARS | 5.2G FIBRE | 19.4G PROTEIN | 2.4G SALT

BAKED SEA BASS WITH WHITE BEAN PURÉE

Sea bass has a divinely delicate flavour and this simple dish – served with cherry tomatoes and bean purée – is devised to sensitively complement the fish.

SERVES: 4
PREP: 20 MINS COOK: 15 MINS

2 tbsp olive oil
1 tbsp fresh thyme leaves
4 large sea bass fillets, about 175 g/6 oz each
salt and pepper (optional)
24 cherry tomatoes, to serve

WHITE BEAN PURÉE
3 tbsp olive oil
2 garlic cloves, chopped
800 g/1 lb 12 oz canned cannellini or butter beans, drained and rinsed
juice of 1 lemon
2–3 tbsp water
4 tbsp chopped fresh flat–leaf parsley
salt and pepper (optional)

1. Preheat the oven to 200°C/400°F/Gas Mark 6. Mix together the oil, thyme and salt and pepper to taste, if using, in a small bowl. Arrange the sea bass fillets on a baking tray, pour over the oil mixture and carefully turn to coat well. Put the tray on the top shelf of the preheated oven and bake for 15 minutes.

2. Meanwhile, make the white bean purée. Heat the oil in a saucepan over a medium heat, add the garlic and cook, stirring, for 1 minute. Add the beans and heat through for 3–4 minutes, then add the lemon juice and salt and pepper to taste, if using. Transfer to a food processor or blender, add the water and process lightly until you have a purée. Alternatively, mash thoroughly with a fork. Stir the parsley into the purée.

3. Serve the sea bass fillets immediately, on top of the warm white bean purée with a drizzle of any pan juices and the cherry tomatoes.

DID YOU KNOW?
Dicentrarchus labrax, the European sea bass, is the variety of bass eaten in the UK and it is one of the most widely eaten across Mediterranean countries. In Greece it is called 'lavraki' – a word that also means a catch that is prized.

PER SERVING: 563 KCALS | 32G FAT | 6G SAT FAT | 19G CARBS | 4G SUGARS | 10G FIBRE | 44G PROTEIN | 0.3G SALT

PRAWN JAMBALAYA

Jambalaya, a traditional Creole dish from New Orleans, has various guises, with the main ingredient varying from chicken and crayfish to prawns and ham.

SERVES: 10
PREP: 25 MINS COOK: 35–45 MINS

2 tbsp vegetable oil
2 onions, roughly chopped
1 green pepper, deseeded and roughly chopped
2 celery sticks, roughly chopped
3 garlic cloves, finely chopped
2 tsp paprika
300 g/10½ oz skinless, boneless chicken breasts, chopped
100 g/3½ oz gluten-free sausages, chopped
3 tomatoes, peeled and chopped
450 g/1 lb long-grain rice
900 ml/1½ pints gluten-free chicken stock or fish stock
1 tsp dried oregano
2 bay leaves
12 large raw prawns, peeled and deveined
4 spring onions, finely chopped
salt and pepper (optional)
2 tbsp chopped fresh flat-leaf parsley, to garnish

1. Heat the oil in a large frying pan over a low heat. Add the onions, green pepper, celery and garlic and cook for 8–10 minutes, until all the vegetables have softened.

2. Stir in the paprika and cook for a further 30 seconds. Add the chicken and sausages and cook for 8–10 minutes, or until lightly browned. Add the tomatoes and cook for 2–3 minutes, or until they have collapsed.

3. Add the rice to the pan and stir well. Pour in the stock, then add the oregano and bay leaves and stir well. Cover and simmer for 10 minutes.

4. Add the prawns and stir. Re-cover and cook for a further 6–8 minutes, or until the rice is tender and the chicken and prawns are cooked through.

5. Stir in the spring onions and season to taste with salt and pepper, if using. Remove and discard the bay leaves, garnish with parsley and serve immediately.

POWER PRAWNS
Prawns provide a rich source of high-quality protein, as well as a range of essential vitamins and minerals – such as iron, selenium and zinc – for those following a healthy diet. They are also notably low in calories.

PER SERVING: 755 KCALS | 1G FAT | 3.8G SAT FAT | 108G CARBS | 7.3G SUGARS | 5.6G FIBRE | 43.2G PROTEIN | 4.9G SALT

PAN-COOKED ROAST CHICKEN

A pan-cooked chicken has all the same flavours as a traditional roast bird,
it's just that all the culinary magic happens in the same pot.

SERVES: 4
PREP: 25–30 MINS COOK: 25–30 MINS

2 tbsp olive oil, plus extra if needed
1 small onion, chopped
450 g/1 lb Brussels sprouts, quartered
450 g/1 lb small, red–skinned new potatoes, quartered
12 baby carrots, peeled but left whole
1 fennel bulb, sliced into small wedges
4 skinned chicken legs (thighs and drumsticks)
4 tbsp gluten–free mustard
4 tbsp clear honey
1 tbsp gluten–free white wine vinegar
2 tsp garlic purée
1 tsp salt
$1/4$–$1/2$ tsp cayenne pepper
50 ml/2 fl oz gluten–free chicken stock
1 tbsp fresh oregano leaves
50 ml/2 fl oz gluten–free dry white wine

1. Preheat the oven to 240°C/475°F/Gas Mark 9. Heat the oil in a large, ovenproof frying pan. Add the onion, sprouts, potatoes, carrots and fennel.

2. Season the chicken with salt and pepper, if using. Push the vegetables to the side of the pan. If necessary, add a little more oil to the pan. Add the chicken to the pan and cook for 2–3 minutes until brown on one side, then turn.

3. Meanwhile, combine the mustard, honey, vinegar, garlic purée, 1 teaspoon of salt, the cayenne pepper and stock in a bowl. Spoon the mixture over the turned chicken pieces to coat well. Drizzle the remaining sauce over the vegetables. Scatter the oregano over the chicken and vegetables.

4. Transfer the pan to the preheated oven and cook for about 20 minutes, or until the vegetables are tender and the chicken is cooked through (the juices should run clear when the thickest part of the meat is pierced with a skewer). Remove the pan from the oven and pour in the wine, stirring the vegetables and deglazing the pan. Serve immediately.

MARINATE IN MUSTARD
To add extra flavour to this dish, make the mustard sauce the day before and then leave the chicken to marinate in the sauce overnight.

PER SERVING: 471 KCALS | 13.1G FAT | 2.3G SAT FAT | 56.6G CARBS | 24.2G SUGARS | 10.1G FIBRE | 34.2G PROTEIN | 2.5G SALT

MEXICAN CHICKEN WITH RICE

The pickled serrano or the chillies used in this recipe give it a gentle kick, but that doesn't take any of the comfort out of eating this much-loved dish.

SERVES: 4
PREP: 25 MINS COOK: 1¼ HOURS

6 skinless chicken thighs on the bone,
about 800 g/1 lb 12 oz total weight
1 litre/1¾ pints water
400 g/14 oz canned chopped tomatoes
2 bay leaves
2 pickled serrano or jalapeño chillies, chopped
2 limes, sliced
1 onion, halved
1 tbsp Mexican oregano
2 tsp ancho chilli powder
2 tsp ground coriander
2 tsp ground cumin
300 g/10½ oz easy-cook, long-grain rice
salt and pepper (optional)

TO SERVE (OPTIONAL)
4 tbsp chopped fresh coriander
2 avocados, peeled, stoned, diced
and tossed with lime juice
other accompaniments of your choice, such as pitted
black olives, plain soya yogurt, chopped cherry
tomatoes and chopped jalapeño peppers

1. Put the chicken and water into a saucepan and slowly bring to the boil, skimming the surface as necessary. When the foam stops rising, stir in the tomatoes, bay leaves, chillies, lime slices, onion, oregano, chilli powder, ground coriander and cumin, and season to taste with salt and pepper, if using. Adjust the heat so the liquid just bubbles, then leave to bubble for about 1 hour until the liquid evaporates and the meat is very tender. The juices should run clear when a skewer is inserted into the thickest part of the meat.

2. Meanwhile, cook the rice according to the packet instructions, then drain well and keep hot.

3. Use a slotted spoon to transfer the chicken mixture to a bowl. Remove the bones and use two forks to shred the meat. Adjust the seasoning, if necessary.

4. To serve, divide the rice between four warmed bowls, then top with the shredded chicken. Sprinkle with chopped coriander and serve with the remaining accompaniments in small bowls for adding at the table.

MEXICAN OREGANO
Oregano has two main forms: Mediterranean and Mexican. The Mexican version has a similar basic flavour to Mediterranean oregano, with the notable addition of citrus and mild liquorice flavours.

PER SERVING: 642 KCALS | 17.8G FAT | 4.5G SAT FAT | 77G CARBS | 7.3G SUGARS | 5.6G FIBRE | 44.9G PROTEIN | 2G SALT

CHICKEN CANNELLINI CHILLI

This dish doesn't need the addition of rice or other carbohydrates because the cannellini beans are very filling.

SERVES: 6
PREP: 20–25 MINS COOK: 40 MINS

1 tbsp vegetable oil
1 onion, diced
2 garlic cloves, finely chopped
1 green pepper, deseeded and diced
1 small jalapeño pepper, deseeded and diced
2 tsp gluten-free chilli powder
2 tsp dried oregano
1 tsp ground cumin
1 tsp salt
500 g/1 lb 2 oz canned cannellini beans, drained and rinsed
750 ml/1¼ pints gluten-free chicken stock
450 g/1 lb cooked chicken breasts, shredded
juice of 1 lime
25 g/1 oz chopped fresh coriander

1. Heat the oil in a large, heavy-based saucepan over a medium-high heat. Add the onion, garlic, pepper and jalapeño and cook, stirring occasionally, for about 5 minutes or until soft. Add the chilli powder, oregano, cumin and salt and cook, stirring, for about a further 30 seconds.

2. Add the beans and stock and bring to the boil. Reduce the heat to medium–low and simmer gently, uncovered, for about 20 minutes.

3. Ladle about half of the bean mixture into a blender or food processor and purée. Return the purée to the pan along with the shredded chicken. Simmer for about 10 minutes or until heated through. Just before serving, stir in the lime juice and coriander. Serve immediately.

FILL UP WITH CANNELLINI
These large, white, kidney-shaped beans have a firm texture and nutty flavour. They are packed with protein and are one of the least glycemic beans, providing a slow, steady source of glucose.

PER SERVING: 243 KCALS | 6.3G FAT | 1.6G SAT FAT | 16.3G CARBS | 2.8G SUGARS | 6.5G FIBRE | 30.1G PROTEIN | 2.2G SALT

BARBECUE-GLAZED SPARE RIBS

The best part of barbecue-glazed spare ribs is the primeval joy of tucking into them. Listed here as optional, a crisp green salad will add both colour and texture.

SERVES: 4

PREP: 20 MINS COOK: 1¼ HOURS

2 racks pork spare ribs, about 800 g/1 lb 12 oz each
3 tbsp instant coffee granules, dissolved in 6 tbsp hot water
6 tbsp gluten-free tomato ketchup
2 tbsp vegetable oil
3 tbsp gluten-free Worcestershire sauce
3 tbsp gluten-free mango chutney
salt and pepper (optional)
crisp green salad, to serve (optional)

1. Put the racks of ribs into a large saucepan and cover with water. Bring to the boil, skim off any scum from the surface, then simmer for 25 minutes.

2. Lift the ribs out of the water and place on a metal rack set over a large roasting tin. Preheat the oven to 190°C/375°F/ Gas Mark 5.

3. Put the coffee, tomato ketchup, oil, Worcestershire sauce and chutney into a bowl and mix together. Season to taste with salt and pepper, if using.

4. Liberally brush the coffee glaze over the racks of ribs. Roast in the preheated oven for 45 minutes, basting occasionally, until the glaze is sticky and lightly charred in places and the ribs are tender.

5. Serve the glazed ribs immediately with salad on the side, if using.

PORK PROTEIN
Pork is a good source of protein and contains many other key nutrients – for example, it is very high in potassium, zinc and iron.

PER SERVING: 910 KCALS | 66.8G FAT | 30.9G SAT FAT | 17.3G CARBS | 12.8G SUGARS | 0.4G FIBRE | 66.6G PROTEIN | 3.2G SALT

MEATBALLS WITH TOMATO SAUCE

Meatballs are surprisingly easy to make, and the handmade ones in this dish are a world apart from pre-prepared, store-bought versions.

SERVES: 4
PREP: 20–30 MINS, PLUS MARINATING AND DRYING
COOK: 30 MINS

1 small onion, grated
finely grated rind of 1 large lemon
2 garlic cloves, crushed
2 tsp dried oregano
1 tsp salt
³/₄ tsp pepper
1 large egg white, lightly beaten
500 g/1 lb 2 oz fresh pork mince
250 g/9 oz fresh beef mince
4 tbsp milled chia seeds
1 tbsp chopped fresh flat–leaf parsley and freshly grated Parmesan cheese (optional), to serve

TOMATO SAUCE
800 g/1 lb 12 oz canned chopped tomatoes
5 garlic cloves, crushed
2 tsp dried oregano
150 ml/5 fl oz olive oil
¹/₂ tsp salt

1. First, make the meatballs. In a small bowl mix together the onion, lemon rind, garlic and oregano with the salt, pepper and egg white.

2. Combine the pork and beef in a large bowl. Add the egg white mixture and use a fork to mix together well.

3. Meanwhile, put the tomatoes into a large pan with the garlic and oregano, 4 tablespoons of the oil and the salt. Bring to the boil, then simmer briskly, uncovered, for 30 minutes, until thickened.

4. Divide the meat mixture into 20 balls, rolling them in the palm of your hand until firm.

5. Heat the remaining oil in a large frying pan. Add the meatballs and fry for about 8 minutes, turning frequently, until brown all over. Transfer to kitchen paper to drain, then add to the tomato sauce and simmer for 5 minutes.

6. Transfer the meatballs and sauce to plates, sprinkle with parsley and serve with Parmesan, if using.

DID YOU KNOW?
Often thought of as a vegetable but actually a fruit, tomatoes are one of our most popular foods and come from the same 'nightshade' family as potatoes and aubergines.

PER SERVING: 662 KCALS | 50G FAT | 13G SAT FAT | 10G CARBS | 9G SUGARS | 4G FIBRE | 40.5G PROTEIN | 2.2G SALT

ROAST PORK WITH GINGERED APPLES

A simple, wholesome balance of ingredients, such as those listed here, can create a fulfilling mealtime experience as much as any more complex recipe.

SERVES: 8
PREP: 25 MINS, PLUS CHILLING/MARINATING
COOK: 55 MINS, PLUS RESTING

2 garlic cloves, crushed
4 tbsp gluten-free red wine
2 tbsp soft brown sugar
1 tbsp gluten-free tamari (Japanese soy sauce)
1 tsp sesame oil
½ tsp ground cinnamon
¼ tsp ground cloves
1 star anise, broken into pieces
½ tsp pepper
350 g/12 oz pork fillet
600 g/1 lb 5 oz cooked French beans, to serve

GINGERED APPLES
4 cooking apples, roughly chopped
1 tbsp rice vinegar
1 tbsp soft brown sugar
4 tbsp apple juice
1 tbsp finely chopped fresh ginger

1. In a large bowl combine the garlic, wine, brown sugar, tamari, sesame oil, cinnamon, cloves, star anise and pepper. Add the pork and toss to coat. Cover and refrigerate overnight.

2. Preheat the oven to 190°C/375°F/Gas Mark 5. Heat a non-stick frying pan over a high heat. Remove the pork from the marinade and sear in the hot pan. Cook for about 8 minutes, or until browned on all sides. Transfer the pork to an ovenproof dish and drizzle with half the marinade. Roast in the preheated oven for 15 minutes. Turn the meat, drizzle the remaining marinade over the top and roast for 30 minutes more, or until cooked through (insert a skewer into the centre of the meat and check that there is no pink meat).

3. Meanwhile, make the gingered apples. In a saucepan, combine all the ingredients and cook over a medium-high heat, until the liquid begins to boil. Reduce the heat to medium-low and simmer, stirring occasionally, for about 20 minutes, or until the apples are soft.

4. Remove the pork from the oven and set aside to rest for 5 minutes. Slice the meat and serve with the apples and French beans.

DID YOU KNOW?
Nearly half the fat in lean pork is the healthy mono-unsaturated kind – like that in olive oil – while only a third is saturated.

PER SERVING: 132 KCALS | 2.5G FAT | 0.75G SAT FAT | 15G CARBS | 15G SUGARS | 2G FIBRE | 10G PROTEIN | 0.37G SALT

DESSERTS AND BAKING

FIG AND WATERMELON SALAD

This magical combination of tropical fruit provides a refreshing plate of goodness – you'll feel the sunshine inside and out as you eat it!

SERVES: 4
PREP: 25 MINS, PLUS CHILLING COOK: 10 MINS

1 watermelon, weighing about 1.5 kg/3 lb 5 oz
115 g/4 oz seedless black grapes
4 figs

SYRUP DRESSING
1 lime
juice and grated rind of 1 orange
1 tbsp maple syrup
2 tbsp clear honey

1. Cut the watermelon into quarters and scoop out and discard the seeds. Cut the flesh away from the rind, then chop the flesh into 2.5–cm/1–inch cubes. Place the watermelon cubes in a bowl with the grapes. Cut each fig lengthways into eight wedges and add to the bowl.

2. Grate the lime and mix the rind with the orange juice and rind, maple syrup and honey in a small saucepan. Bring to the boil over a low heat. Pour the mixture over the fruit and stir. Leave to cool. Stir again, cover and chill in the refrigerator for at least 1 hour, stirring occasionally.

3. Divide the fruit salad equally between four bowls and serve.

FIG GOODNESS
Figs have multiple dietary benefits. They are high in natural sugars, minerals and soluble fibre, and rich in minerals such as iron, potassium, calcium and magnesium. They also provide a good source of antioxidant vitamins.

PER SERVING: 222 KCALS | 0.8G FAT | 0.1G SAT FAT | 57.3G CARBS | 48.7G SUGARS | 3.4G FIBRE | 3G PROTEIN | TRACE SALT

RAW FRUIT TART

Flour is not the only way to make a delicious tart – here we've used pecan nuts and dates to create a crunchy base for the fresh fruit topping.

SERVES: 8
PREP: 20 MINS, PLUS SOAKING COOK: NONE

BASE
150 g/5¹⁄₂ oz pecan nuts
55 g/2 oz stoned dates
1 tsp ground cinnamon
1 tbsp vanilla extract
pinch of salt

TOPPING
280 g/10 oz mixed fresh fruit (choose a colourful selection of fresh fruit in season)
juice of ¹⁄₂ a lemon
1 tbsp vanilla extract

CASHEW CREAM
225 g/8 oz cashew nuts
1 tbsp agave nectar
1 tbsp unwaxed lemon juice

1. Soak the cashews for the cashew cream in a bowl of water for approximately 8 hours or overnight.

2. Put all the ingredients for the tart base into the bowl of a food processor fitted with a chopping blade. Process until the nuts are finely chopped and the mixture begins to clump together. Press the mixture into the base of a 20-cm/8-inch pie dish and then use the back of a spoon to smooth it into a firm crust.

3. To make the mixed-fruit topping, you might like to halve strawberries, grapes or blackberries, and core and chop apples or pears. Put the prepared fruit into a large mixing bowl and toss with the lemon juice and vanilla extract. Arrange the fruit over the tart base.

4. To make the cashew cream, drain the soaked cashews and put them into the bowl of a food processor fitted with a chopping blade. Add the agave nectar, lemon juice and 175 ml/6 fl oz of cold water. Blend to a smooth cream and serve immediately with the tart.

CASHEW CREAM
Soaking the cashews makes the cashew cream less grainy but, if time is short, you can skip the soaking and it will still work well.

PER SERVING: 334 KCALS | 27G FAT | 4G SAT FAT | 13G CARBS | 9G SUGARS | 4G FIBRE | 8G PROTEIN | 0.1G SALT

BLUEBERRY AND LIME SAGO DESSERT

The small balls, or pearls, of sago are noteworthy for their very high carbohydrate, low-fibre content and are very easy to digest.

SERVES: 4
PREP: 20–25 MINS, PLUS COOLING AND CHILLING
COOK: 35 MINS

300 ml/10 fl oz coconut milk
300 ml/10 fl oz water
75 g/23/4 oz sago pearls
25 g/1 oz shredded coconut
40 g/11/2 oz caster sugar
grated rind and juice of 1 lime
1 tsp vanilla extract
1/2 tsp ground cinnamon
1/4 tsp grated nutmeg
20 blueberries
60 g/21/4 oz fresh mango, diced

1. Bring the coconut milk and water to the boil in a saucepan over a medium heat. Pour in the sago, stirring with a fork to keep the pearls separate. Turn down the heat and simmer on very low for 20 minutes, stirring frequently to prevent the sago sticking to the pan.

2. Meanwhile, put the coconut in a non-stick frying pan over a high heat, stirring occasionally, for 1 minute, or until it turns golden. Immediately remove from the heat and set aside.

3. When the sago has simmered for 20 minutes, add the sugar, lime rind and half the juice, the vanilla extract and spices. Stir well and simmer for a further 10 minutes, or until the sago pearls are virtually transparent and tender. If the mixture becomes too thick to simmer before the sago is cooked through, add a little boiling water and mix in thoroughly. When the sago is ready, take the pan off the heat and stir in the remaining lime juice. Allow to cool for 10 minutes.

4. Spoon the sago mixture into four stemmed glasses or ramekins and smooth the top with the back of the spoon. Cover and chill for 30 minutes–1 hour. Decorate each dessert with a quarter of the toasted coconut, blueberries and diced mango.

PER SERVING: 280 KCALS | 15G FAT | 13G SAT FAT | 33G CARBS | 15G SUGARS | 2G FIBRE | 1.5G PROTEIN | TRACE SALT

CREAMY COCONUT AND MANGO QUINOA

This is a healthy, easy-to-prepare quinoa mix with coconut, mango, blueberries, lime and ginger as contributing flavours.

SERVES: 4
PREP: 20 MINS, PLUS COOLING AND STANDING
COOK: 20–25 MINS, PLUS STANDING

300 ml/10 fl oz canned coconut milk
115 g/4 oz white quinoa, rinsed
1 large ripe mango, about 550 g/1 lb 4 oz
75 g/2³/₄ oz caster sugar
juice of 1 large lime
4-cm/1½-inch piece fresh ginger, sliced into chunks
100 g/3½ oz blueberries
4 tbsp toasted coconut chips
4 lime wedges, to decorate

1. Put the coconut milk and quinoa into a small saucepan and bring to the boil. Cover and simmer for 15–20 minutes, or until most of the liquid has evaporated. Remove from the heat, but leave covered for a further 10 minutes to allow the grains to swell. Fluff up with a fork, tip into a bowl and leave to cool.

2. Meanwhile, peel the mango, discard the stone and roughly chop the flesh (you will need 350 g/ 12 oz). Put the mango into a food processor with the sugar and lime juice. Squeeze the ginger in a garlic press and add the juice to the mango mixture. Process for 30 seconds to make a smooth purée.

3. Mix the mango mixture into the cooled quinoa and leave to stand for 30 minutes.

4. Divide the mixture between four bowls and sprinkle with the blueberries and coconut chips. Decorate with lime wedges and serve.

BLUE GOODNESS
Blueberries are very low in calories and are among the highest antioxidant value fruits.

PER SERVING: 438 KCALS | 21.5G FAT | 17.4G SAT FAT | 60.1G CARBS | 34G SUGARS | 5.2G FIBRE | 6.9G PROTEIN | TRACE SALT

APPLE AND CINNAMON PIE

An autumn or winter classic, this is a generous showstopper dessert to finish off any family meal or dinner party.

SERVES: 8
PREP: 35 MINS COOK: 30 MINS

PASTRY

60 g/2¼ oz white vegetable shortening
15 g/½ oz gluten–free margarine
225 g/8 oz gluten–free plain flour
1 tbsp gluten–free baking powder
pinch of salt
10 g/¼ oz gluten–free plain flour, for dusting
1 tbsp gluten–free soya milk, for brushing
10 g/¼ oz caster sugar, for sprinkling

FILLING

1 kg/2 lb 4 oz cooking apples, peeled, cored and sliced
150 g/5½ oz caster sugar
2 tsp gluten–free cornflour
1 tbsp ground cinnamon

1. To make the pastry, put the vegetable shortening and margarine into a large mixing bowl. Pour over 100 ml/3½ fl oz of boiling water and mix with a wooden spoon until creamy. Add the flour, baking powder and salt, stir together, then turn out onto a lightly floured work surface and knead together into a smooth ball. Leave the dough to cool for 5 minutes. Roll the dough out on a sheet of clingfilm to a shape that slightly overhangs a 23–cm/9–inch round pie dish. Set aside.

2. Preheat the oven to 180° C/350° F/Gas Mark 4.

3. Place the apples in a large saucepan with the sugar, cornflour and cinnamon, and add 3 tablespoons of water. Cook gently for 5–10 minutes, or until the apple is just tender and most of the liquid in the pan has been thickened by the cornflour. Leave the mixture to cool.

4. Put the apple filling into the pie dish. Lift the pastry on the sheet of clingfilm (to support it) and carefully transfer the pastry to the top of the pie, removing the clingfilm and pressing the edges down to form a crust and trimming away any excess with a sharp knife. Re–roll the trimmings to make decorative leaves and place these on top of the pie.

5. Brush the top of the pie with a little soya milk and sprinkle with a little caster sugar. Bake in the preheated oven for 30 minutes, or until just golden. Serve hot or cold.

PER SERVING: 330 KCALS | 10G FAT | 4G SAT FAT | 55G CARBS | 31G SUGARS | 4G FIBRE | 3.5G PROTEIN | 0.5G SALT

ANGEL FOOD CAKE

You'll feel light as a feather after a piece of this airy cake made with rice flour, tapioca flour and gluten-free cornflour.

MAKES: 1 CAKE
PREP: 15 MINS, PLUS STANDING
COOK: 45 MINS

butter, for greasing
10 egg whites
60 g/2¼ oz white rice flour
60 g/2¼ oz tapioca flour
60 g/2¼ oz gluten-free cornflour
60 g/2¼ oz potato flour
300 g/10½ oz caster sugar
1½ tsp gluten-free cream of tartar
½ tsp vanilla essence
½ tsp salt
500 g/1 lb 2 oz bag of frozen fruits of the forest (optional)
85 g/3 oz caster sugar (optional)
10 g/¼ oz icing sugar, to decorate

1. Preheat the oven to 180°C/350°F/Gas Mark 4. Grease a 20-cm/8-inch cake tin and line with baking paper.

2. Allow the egg whites to sit for approximately 30 minutes at room temperature in a large bowl. In a separate bowl, sift the white rice flour, tapioca flour, cornflour, potato flour and 175 g/6 oz of the sugar.

3. Using a food processor or mixer, whisk the egg whites with the cream of tartar, vanilla essence and salt until soft peaks form. Gradually add the remaining 125 g/4½ oz of sugar until stiff peaks develop. Add the flour mixture and fold in.

4. Spoon the mixture into the prepared tin and bake in the preheated oven for approximately 45 minutes until firm to the touch and a skewer inserted in the centre comes out clean.

5. Remove from the oven and, leaving the cake in the tin, turn upside-down to cool on a wire rack. Poach the fruits of the forest with the caster sugar gently until soft, if using. Allow to cool completely. When the cake is cool, remove from the tin and decorate with icing sugar and the drained mixed fruit, if desired.

TURN TO TAPIOCA
Tapioca flour is a starchy white flour with a gentle, sweet flavour. It is used as an alternative to traditional wheat flours.

PER CAKE: 2784 KCALS | 7G FAT | 3G SAT FAT | 618G CARBS | 419G SUGARS | 25G FIBRE | 50G PROTEIN | 4.1G SALT

PISTACHIO MACAROONS

A delicious gluten-free option, pistachios are a good source of fibre and protein and can help to lower cholesterol and prevent cardiovascular disease.

MAKES: 24
PREP: 25 MINS, PLUS COOLING COOK: 20 MINS

55 g/2 oz skinned pistachio nuts, plus extra
to decorate
40 g/1½ oz icing sugar
1 tbsp rice flour
2 egg whites
55 g/2 oz caster sugar
55 g/2 oz desiccated coconut
1 tbsp chopped fresh mint

1. Preheat the oven to 180°C/350°F/Gas Mark 4. Line two baking trays with baking paper.

2. Place the pistachio nuts, icing sugar and rice flour in a food processor and process until finely ground.

3. Whisk the egg whites in a clean, dry bowl until stiff, then gradually whisk in the caster sugar. Fold in the pistachio mixture, coconut and mint.

4. Place spoonfuls of the mixture onto the prepared baking trays and press a pistachio on top of each to decorate.

5. Bake in the preheated oven for about 20 minutes, until firm and just beginning to brown. Cool on the baking tray and serve.

DID YOU KNOW?
Pistachios – originally from Turkey and the Middle East – get their green colour from chlorophyll, the same chemical found in leaves. It's this that makes pistachios such a good source of carotenes.

PER SERVING: 37 KCALS | 2.5G FAT | 1.5G SAT FAT | 2.5G CARBS | 2G SUGARS | 0.4G FIBRE | 1G PROTEIN | TRACE SALT

LEMON MERINGUE COOKIES

*These light, chewy cookies are a delicious treat when served with coffee.
The lemon juice helps to stabilize the meringue.*

SERVES: 8
PREP: 20–25 MINS, PLUS COOLING   COOK: 1½ HOURS

2 large egg whites
⅛ tsp gluten-free cream of tartar
pinch of salt
140 g/5 oz caster sugar
finely grated zest of 1 lemon

1. Preheat the oven to 110°C/225°F/Gas Mark ¼. Line a large baking sheet with baking paper.

2. In a large, greasefree bowl, beat the egg whites with an electric mixer until they are frothy. Add the cream of tartar and salt and continue to beat on high until soft peaks form. Gradually add the sugar and continue to beat on high for about 3–4 minutes or until stiff peaks form. Fold in the lemon zest.

3. Drop the mixture in rounded teaspoons onto the prepared baking sheet. Bake in the preheated oven for about 1½ hours, or until dry and crisp but not yet beginning to colour. Turn off the oven and leave the cookies inside the oven for a further 30 minutes. Serve at room temperature.

MERINGUES TO HAND
Meringues store well in an airtight container,
so make them in advance for unexpected guests!

PER SERVING: 73 KCALS | TRACE FAT | TRACE SAT FAT | 17.7G CARBS | 17.6G SUGARS | 0.1G FIBRE | 0.9G PROTEIN | 0.3G SALT

CLEMENTINE ALMOND CAKE

There's no escaping either the smell or the taste of clementines in this spongey, gluten-free cake – and the curd cheese topping adds extra luxury.

SERVES: 10
PREP: 20 MINS COOK: 30 MINS

125 g/4½ oz unsalted butter, plus extra for greasing
125 g/4½ oz caster sugar
4 eggs, separated
150 g/5½ oz millet flour
2 tsp gluten-free baking powder
125 g/4½ oz ground almonds
juice and finely grated rind of 2 clementines

SYRUP

juice of 4 clementines
100 g/3½ oz caster sugar

TOPPING

225 g/8 oz low-fat soft curd cheese or quark
2 tbsp sugar
2 tbsp extra-thick double cream

1. Preheat the oven to 180°C/ 350°F/Gas Mark 4. Grease a 23–cm/9–inch springform cake tin.

2. Beat together the butter and sugar for 3 minutes, until fluffy. Gradually beat in the egg yolks.

3. Combine the flour, baking powder and ground almonds, then beat into the butter, sugar and egg yolk mixture. Mix in the clementine juice, reserving the rind.

4. Whisk the egg whites until they hold stiff peaks. Fold carefully into the mixture using a large metal spoon. Spoon the batter into the prepared tin.

5. Bake in the preheated oven for 30–40 minutes, until a skewer inserted into the centre comes out clean.

6. Meanwhile, to make the syrup, put the clementine juice and sugar into a small saucepan, bring to the boil. Boil for 3 minutes, until syrupy.

7. With the cake still in its tin, make holes all over the surface with a skewer. Pour over the hot syrup. When it has trickled into the holes, remove the cake from the tin and transfer to a wire rack to cool completely.

8. To make the topping, beat together the curd cheese, sugar and cream. Spread over the cake and sprinkle with the reserved clementine rind.

PER SERVING: 392 KCALS | 21G FAT | 9G SAT FAT | 39G CARBS | 27.2G SUGARS | 0G FIBRE | 10.6G PROTEIN | 0.4G SALT

FRUIT SODA BREAD

Soda bread might sound like a workaday choice, but add prunes, apricots, apples, cranberries, maple syrup and pumpkin seeds and it becomes a must-have luxury.

MAKES: 1 LOAF
PREP: 25 MINS, PLUS STANDING   COOK: 25–30 MINS

55 g/2 oz ready-to-eat stoned
prunes, chopped
55 g/2 oz ready-to-eat dried
apricots, chopped
40 g/1½ oz ready-to-eat dried
apples, chopped
40 g/1½ oz dried cranberries
150 ml/5 fl oz pure apple juice
450 g/1 lb gluten-free plain flour
1½ tbsp gluten-free baking powder
2 tsp xanthan gum
¼ tsp salt
2 tbsp sunflower oil, plus extra for greasing
225 ml/8 fl oz milk, plus extra for brushing
4 tbsp maple syrup
1 tbsp pumpkin seeds
butter, to serve (optional)

1. Place the prunes, apricots, apples and cranberries in a bowl and pour over the apple juice. Cover and leave to stand for about 30 minutes.

2. Preheat the oven to 200°C/400°F/Gas Mark 6. Brush a baking tray with oil. Sift the flour, baking powder, xanthan gum and salt into a bowl and make a well in the centre.

3. Mix the oil, milk and maple syrup and add to the dry ingredients with the fruits and juice, mixing lightly to a soft, but not sticky, dough. Add a little more milk if the dough feels dry.

4. Shape the dough to a smooth round on the prepared baking tray, flatten slightly and cut a deep cross through the centre almost to the base. Gently pull the wedges apart at the points. Brush with milk and sprinkle with pumpkin seeds.

5. Bake in the preheated oven for 25–30 minutes, or until golden brown and the base sounds hollow when tapped. Serve in chunks with butter, if desired.

PUMPKIN MAGIC
Pumpkin seeds are rich in monounsaturated fatty acids – these help to lower your blood's supply of bad LDL cholesterol and increase the good HDL cholesterol.

PER LOAF: 2788 KCALS | 48.7G FAT | 6.2G SAT FAT | 557.4G CARBS | 164.1G SUGARS | 25.6G FIBRE | 36.4G PROTEIN | 8G SALT

QUINOA AND CHIVE ROLLS

These rolls provide the perfect gluten-free accompaniment for a soup or, combined with the filling of your choice, a wholesome lunchtime snack.

MAKES: 8
PREP: 25 MINS, PLUS RISING AND COOLING
COOK: 20–25 MINS

200 g/7 oz buckwheat flour
150 g/5½ oz potato flour
2 tsp xanthan gum
1½ tsp salt
7 g/¼ oz easy-blend dried yeast
100 g/3½ oz cooked quinoa
3 tbsp snipped chives
350 ml/12 fl oz tepid water
1 small egg, beaten
1 tbsp olive oil, plus extra for brushing
15 ml/1 tbsp milk, for glazing

1. Brush a large baking sheet with oil.

2. Sift the buckwheat flour, potato flour, xanthan gum and salt together into a bowl, then stir in the yeast, quinoa and chives.

3. Make a well in the centre and stir in the water, egg and oil to make a soft dough. Very lightly knead the dough until smooth.

4. Divide the dough into eight pieces and shape each piece into a smooth ball. Arrange on the prepared baking sheet, cover and leave in a warm place for about 1 hour, or until doubled in size. Meanwhile, preheat the oven to 200°C/400°F/ Gas Mark 6.

5. Brush the rolls with milk to glaze. Bake in the preheated oven for 20–25 minutes, or until firm and golden brown. Transfer to a wire rack to cool.

NUTTY QUINOA
Quinoa is rich in protein and has a pleasantly nutty taste that works well in bakes and breads.

PER SERVING: 200 KCALS | 4.2G FAT | 0.7G SAT FAT | 36.4G CARBS | 1.3G SUGARS | 4.3G FIBRE | 6.1G PROTEIN | 1.2G SALT

CARAMELIZED RED ONION, THYME AND OLIVE FOCACCIA

Once you've used it a few times, this recipe is easy to adapt — you can combine rosemary with thyme, or add a combination of your favourite herbs.

MAKES: 1 LOAF
PREP: 30 MINS, PLUS RISING   COOK: 30–35 MINS

butter, for greasing
450 g/1 lb gluten–free, wheat–free
white bread flour
2 tsp dried yeast
2 tsp caster sugar
350 ml/12 fl oz tepid milk
2 eggs, beaten
1 garlic clove, finely chopped
10–12 black olives, stoned and halved
rock salt (optional)
cracked black pepper (optional)
grated Parmesan cheese, for sprinkling (optional)

CARAMELISED ONION
50 g/1³/₄ oz butter
2 small red onions, thinly sliced
4–5 sprigs thyme

1. To make the caramelised onion, melt the butter in a small frying pan and fry the onions and thyme gently until the onions are soft and caramelised. Remove from the heat and cool until required.

2. Grease a 25– x 35–cm/10– x 14–inch baking tray and line with baking paper.

3. Sift the flour into a bowl. In a separate bowl, mix the yeast, sugar and tepid milk and leave to stand for 5–10 minutes at room temperature until frothy. Mix in the eggs, add the liquid mixture to the flour and mix well.

4. Transfer the dough onto the prepared tray, pushing it out to the edges. Cover with a clean damp tea towel and leave for about 45 minutes until it has doubled in size. Preheat the oven to 180°C/350°F/Gas Mark 4.

5. Spread the caramelised onion over the top of the bread, sprinkle with the garlic, olives, salt, pepper and Parmesan, if using. Press the toppings lightly into the bread using your fingers.

6. Bake in the preheated oven for 30–35 minutes until golden and crusty. Remove from the oven and leave to cool on a wire rack. The bread can be served hot or cold.

PER LOAF: 2534 KCALS | 81.5G FAT | 42G SAT FAT | 394G CARBS | 41G SUGARS | 8G FIBRE | 52G PROTEIN | 6.1G SALT

INDEX